NONVERBAL

SELLING

POWER

NONVERBAL
SELLING
POWER

by **Gerhard Gschwandtner**
with **Pat Garnett**

Prentice Hall, Inc.

Englewood Cliffs, New Jersey

Prentice-Hall International, Inc., *London*
Prentice-Hall of Australia, Pty, Ltd., *Sydney*
Prentice-Hall Canada, Inc., *Toronto*
Prentice-Hall of India Private, Ltd., *New Delhi*
Prentice-Hall of Japan, Inc., *Tokyo*
Prentice-Hall of Southeast Asia Pte, Ltd., *Singapore*
Whitehall Books, Ltd., Wellington, *New Zealand*
Editora Prentice-Hall do Brasil Ltda., *Rio de Janeiro*
Prentice-Hall Hispanoamericana, S.A., *Mexico*

© 1985 *by*
Prentice-Hall, Inc.
Englewood Cliffs, New Jersey

Second Printing.....May 1987

Library of Congress Cataloging in Publication Data

Gschwandtner, Gerhard.
  Nonverbal selling power.

  Bibliography: p.
  1. Selling—Psychological aspects.   2. Nonverbal
communication (Psychology)   I. Garnett, Pat.   II. Title.
HF5438.8.P75G79   1985   658.8'5   85-6358

ISBN 0-13-623455-0

ISBN 0-13-623448-8 {PBK}

This book is dedicated to all salespeople
who have good eyesight but cannot see.

ACKNOWLEDGMENTS

I wish to express my sincere thanks to the photographer Bill Sharp, who shot over 3,000 pictures for the preparation of this book. The participating cast of Doug Tillet, Betsy Ames, Doug Roberts, Jim Scopeletis, John Healey, Frank Steogerer, and Caron Tate created the appropriate nonverbal expressions exclusively in response to feeling and attitude directions. Without their skills, this book would not exist. Their work laid the foundation for the best-selling audio-visual sales training course "The Languages of Selling" (over 30,000 people from over 900 companies have completed the course). This course and the resulting field experience have become the basis for this book.

Special thanks go to Pat Garnett, the Associate Editor of *Personal Selling Power*, for organizing, condensing, and rewriting the enormous amount of information on the subject collected over the past ten years.

I further wish to thank the entire staff of *Personal Selling Power* for their enthusiastic cooperation on this project.

Gerhard Gschwandtner

Foreword

This book will show you how you can use nonverbal communication techniques together with professional selling skills for increased sales results. Nonverbal communication is a vital part of the sales process. History provides a dramatic example of how self-enhancing gestures and postures can lead to victory:

> After the legendary televised debate between the presidential candidates Richard Nixon and John F. Kennedy, the majority of the TV audience found Kennedy far superior to Nixon. The majority of the radio audience, however, judged Richard Nixon the winner of the debate.

In selling, many salespeople are still at the level of the candidate who had to learn about nonverbal communication through the school of hard knocks. Although most salespeople know how to say the right things, they often lose the sale because of self-defeating nonverbal expressions. They're losing sales while their seemingly less knowledgeable colleagues get more orders.

Dr. Albert Mehrabian, professor of psychology at UCLA, put things into perspective when he found that our feelings and attitudes are communicated only 7 percent with words, but 38 percent with tone of voice, and 55 percent nonverbally. This bit of scientific information should not lead you to conclude that in order to learn how to use nonverbal selling power you need to become a psychologist. That's not necessary. Remember, the objective in selling is to get the order (and create more satisfied customers), not to walk away with a psychological profile of your prospects.

This book cannot teach you the exact psychological meaning of a single posture or gesture. This would be self-defeating (there are over 10,000 hand gestures alone!) and unnecessary. The pictures in this book will show you the most important nonverbal expressions you will find in a selling situation and what they mean in terms of your selling strategy. With the use of a simple traffic light model, we'll divide all nonverbal expressions into three major signals that will tell you how to respond to a prospect's hidden feelings and attitudes *before* they can become a real threat to your selling efforts.

But reading a prospect's nonverbal expressions is only half the secret to more sales. This book doesn't stop there. You'll also learn specific ways for improving your own nonverbal selling power. Discover how you can enhance your sales presentation with effective nonverbal techniques throughout the call, from the opening to the close.

CONTENTS

PART I

10. Closing *(continued)*

Action—Future Action Close
Action—Customer as Sales Assistant Close
Action—Change of Scene Close
Action—Pack-Up and Leave Close

NONVERBAL
SELLING
POWER

PART I

Learning Nonverbal
Selling Power

CHAPTER 1

The Importance of
Nonverbal Communication

During an average 30-minute sales call, buyer and seller exchange approximately 800 different nonverbal messages. Think about your last meeting with a client. Can you recall his or her basic sitting position? Did he lean forward or backward in his chair? You may have seen her smile, but did you notice whether her arms and legs were crossed at the same time?

Most salespeople focus on the verbal part of the sale. Some of them listen to the tone of voice—*how* the words are said. And the salespeople who pay attention to body language focus almost exclusively on facial expressions. Obviously, these are all necessary areas of interest. Words, the way they're spoken, and a person's face all give the seller information about how the call is going.

Dr. Albert Mehrabian, a noted researcher in the field of nonverbal communication (UCLA), found that only 7 percent of our feelings and attitudes are communicated with words, 38 percent via tone of voice and a whopping 55 percent through nonverbal expressions. These numbers are astonishing. But that's only part of the picture. As the graph of Figure 1-1 indicates, the communication channels over which we have the most control, and understand the best, have the least amount of impact. And the channels over which we have the least control, and understand the least, have the most impact.

3

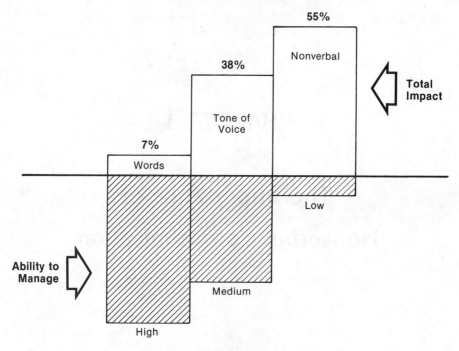

FIGURE 1-1

Impact means the degree of importance a channel of communication has on the outcome of the sale. The following example will show you how vital nonverbal cues are to successful selling.

Tom, a salesman, enters his client's office, smiles, shakes hands, and sits down. He gives his presentation, asks for the order, is turned down, and leaves.

From this description, you can't tell why things didn't go well for Tom. Even if you were able to read a typed transcript of *what* Tom and his client said to each other, you probably wouldn't know.

Only if we show you a videotape of nonverbal cues and messages will Tom's failure become clear. The video recording shows the following scene:

Tom enters the office slowly. He is tired and nervous. He offers his hand limply, holding his briefcase in front of him. His client uncrosses his arms, stands up but remains behind his desk, returns the unenthusiastic handshake, and indicates that Tom should take a seat across from him, on the opposite side of the desk.

Tom knows his presentation fairly well, but he feels that his client is unreceptive, so he looks down at his hands and his brochures, avoiding eye contact with his client. While Tom gives his presentation, the client becomes increasingly bored and annoyed. He fiddles with a paper weight on his desk, then leans back, crosses his arms while closing his hands into fists, and crosses his legs, shifting away from Tom.

When Tom finally looks at his client, he sees the mask of a smile, feels uncertain about how to proceed, and asks for the order. With a sigh, the client says that his company is not ready to make such a large purchase right now. He rises, offers his hand, and then motions to the door.

During this sales call there were hundreds of other nonverbal signals exchanged by both Tom and his client. Each of them reacted to the other's signals, mirrored the other's negative messages, and concluded the call feeling as if he'd wasted his time. That much is certainly true. But it didn't have to happen that way. Tom could have managed his own nonverbal communication and influenced his client's behavior simply by planning his body language as well as his words.

THREE STAGES TO INCREASED NONVERBAL SELLING POWER

Reading a prospect's body language is not the only goal in mastering nonverbal communication. The learning pyramid (Figure 1-2) illustrates the three separate stages of awareness and skill necessary before you become an expert in verbal and nonverbal selling power.

Stage I, Awareness of the Buyer, involves learning the five major nonverbal communication channels and how to interpret the buyer's nonverbal signals. Chapter 2 describes these channels in detail. Basically, they

FIGURE 1-2

represent a shorthand system of scanning the buyer for clusters of gestures. Instead of looking for specific movements or postures that "mean" the client is bored, defensive, or angry, a group of gestures from the five channels can be classified into one of three types of signals.

Green signals indicate that your buyer is open and receptive to your presentation. Yellow signals indicate obstacles to your strategy and warn you to exercise caution. The hidden obstacle must be uncovered before moving on with the sale. Red signals alert you to stop and redirect your sales approach. This traffic light model, fully explained in Chapter 3, will increase your knowledge of the buyer. But it won't teach you about your own nonverbal communication patterns or enhance your selling power until you move through the next two stages.

Stage II, Awareness of Self, is tremendously important. Your own nonverbal expressions can make or break a sale. Ask yourself: "How can I communicate in order to enhance the impact of my verbal selling skills? How am I perceived by the buyer? How can I avoid communicating self-defeating nonverbal signals during the call?"

This stage requires role-playing and practice. Constructive criticism from peers and videotaping yourself in mock sales situations will show you how you look and act when your mind is on what you're saying. Once you understand your own nonverbal behavior, and how you use it to interact with clients, you are ready for the next step.

Stage III, Management of Self and Buyer, is the ultimate goal of nonverbal selling power to use at every call. To reach this stage, you need to develop the ability to consistently apply nonverbal communication techniques together with professional selling skills. This means combining the new techniques with your existing verbal selling skills. Continued role-playing and observation of the buyer and yourself will give you the ability to:

- spot negative nonverbal signals early in the sale;
- respond faster and more accurately to the buyer's nonverbal signals;
- increase your "fluency" in managing your own nonverbal expressions;
- increase your ability to combine verbal and nonverbal skills.

Body language reflects people's true feelings when they are unaware of their gestures. Your clients are visually telling you when they are uncertain, need more information, want a chance to ask questions, or have strong objections—it's all in plain sight. And so are your responses. You may "mirror" their emotions by making similar gestures, or take on a defensive posture in response to an objection. If they ask a question, and you feel uncertain about how to answer, your body will be the messenger of your uncertainty.

Once you are *aware* of the buyer and *aware* of yourself, you can put nonverbal selling power to work for you by managing your own and your client's body language.

How can you do this? By responding, instead of reacting, to your client's messages. By being friendly and positive, reassuring and understanding, both verbally and nonverbally. Use all 100 percent of your communications power by using the 55 percent of the message you send without opening your mouth.

SEEING IS BELIEVING

If you are still skeptical about the importance of nonverbal communication, try the following exercise. Look at each of the following photographs and give the salesman a rating of poor, fair, or good. Then list three reasons why you got that impression.

The first photo shows the salesman acting as a passive listener. He could improve his nonverbal signals by leaning forward, unclasping his hands, placing his feet flat and closer to himself, and sitting farther forward in the chair. His expression is rather bland—there's no enthusiasm here! At least he is not sending out any negative signals. A client would rate him as average at best.

The second photo shows the salesman in a very unfavorable position. His arms and feet are crossed in a defensive manner. In addition, his legs and body are oriented away from his client (and probably pointed in the direction of the door). His expression also suggests confrontation. He won't get through his presentation before he is asked to leave.

The third photo shows the salesman in an active, positive posture. He is leaning forward, displays an open-handed gesture and is using good eye contact, giving the impression of friendliness and concern. His legs are open and his feet are flat on the floor suggesting cooperation and stability. This salesman is about to close the sale.

You probably had no difficulty deciding on the ratings. But could you put into writing why you made those choices? Perhaps you hesitated over the poor rating because the salesman was reacting to the negative behavior of his client. This brings out an important point. The worst thing a seller can do is mimic a buyer's negative signals or react to the client with anything but positive, helpful nonverbal messages.

The body language of failure = no eye contact, fidgeting, nervousness, defensiveness or confrontation, and poor posture. Your client will interpret these nonverbal messages as fear, weakness, or discontent.

The body language of success = good eye contact, a firm, loose, erect body posture, and open gestures that move toward the buyer. These signals give the impression of power, confidence, and satisfaction.

AN EXAMPLE OF FAILURE AND SUCCESS

When Dan Rather replaced Walter Cronkite as anchorman for the CBS Evening News, success seemed inevitable. He brought impeccable credentials—five Emmys and a rating as best White House correspondent in the history of broadcasting—and an extremely telegenic face, to his new post.

Yet CBS began to drop in the ratings, finally settling into third and last place, after Cronkite's departure. Viewers were polled to discover what types of impressions they were getting from Rather in comparison to Cronkite by picking adjectives from the following list, in the hopes of understanding the audience's unexpected negative reactions.

cold	warm
rigid	flexible
hard sell	soft sell
aggressive	conciliatory
self-oriented	other-oriented
seeks attention	seeks privacy
workaholic	balanced life
superior	equal
tense	relaxed

Most people picked words from the left column to describe Rather and words from the right one to describe Cronkite. The problem was Rather's failure to adapt his body language to his new role. As an aggressive reporter, his role required firmness and an impression of urgency and tension. But as anchorman, he needed to convey friendliness and a relaxed attitude.

So the remaking of Rather's nonverbal image began, and was a success. His changes included:

1. **Body movements**: his slight left to right movements, communicating insecurity or doubt which often went to a controlled position, making him appear rigid and tense, were altered. He began more forward and backward motions indicating a free discharge of drive and energy.

2. **Facial expressions**: his limited variety of emotions seemed mechanical and he ended the newscast with serious or stilted expressions. After some coaching from CBS, Rather's face came alive with a broader range of emotions and his general rate of smiling increased.

3. **Eye movements**: too many eye-down movements communicated a preoccupation with his script which made him appear removed, cold, and concerned with facts—not people. Increased eye contact with the camera and use of the teleprompter made Rather seem more human.

4. **Arm postures**: keeping his arms close to his side, or one arm pressed heavily against the desk gave the impression of Rather as overly controlled and tense. An increase in hand motions and arm movement gave Rather a more relaxed appearance and made his stories seem faster paced.

Dan Rather changed his image from a public defender to a public servant by altering his nonverbal signals. As a salesperson, you can project an image similar to a news show anchorman's. Check the list of descriptive adjectives once more. How many words in the left column describe your sales approach? Trust is a major factor in a buyer's decision to purchase your product or service. Whom would you rather buy from—a hard-news reporter or Walter Cronkite?

BODY LANGUAGE—SALES HYPE OR SELLING STRATEGY?

With the appearance of popular books on body language, nonverbal communication began to move out of the universities and research labs into average people's lives. About the same time, it started to get a bad reputation. Nobody wanted to believe that their inner emotions could be "read" by others; that their bodies were letting out their deep dark secrets.

So the criticism began. Nonverbal communication was called silly, stupid, ridiculous, and a waste of time. People asked: "How can anyone remember what thousands of gestures mean?" The problem was that many books gave the impression that each gesture had its own meaning and was the same for all people in all situations. This simply isn't true. Let's take arm crossing as an example. Cross your arms. How do you feel? Defensive? Closed-minded? Probably not. That's because there has to be a *reason* for crossing your arms.

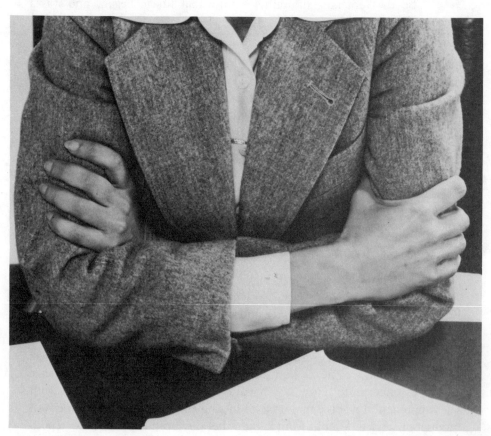

If you go into a client's office, and her arms are already crossed, notice the room temperature. She might just be cold! Or she may have just gotten off the phone with her boss and he was chewing her out. Maybe she's thinking about the argument she had with her spouse last night. The point is this: you can't attribute her gesture to your being there until she does something in reaction to something you do or say. Once you've started your presentation and she suddenly crosses her arms you can be fairly certain that you caused that reaction. This is the time to stop what you're doing and find out why.

BODY LANGUAGE ISN'T NEW

Understanding the power of nonverbal communication will put you in excellent company. Man has used gestures since he appeared on earth. The Greeks were quite familiar with interpreting a man's character by watching how he carried himself and expressed his ideas with his body. No one in this country needs to tell us what it means when someone gives us the finger. But in France, no one would be able to understand what point you're trying to get across. So not all gestures are universal.

The following quotes will make you aware of how widespread man's knowledge of body language has been over the years.

"Your face, my thane, is as a book where men
May read strange matters. To beguile the time,
Look like the time; bear welcome in your eye,
Your hand, your tongue: look like the innocent flower,
But be the serpent under't."

SHAKESPEARE *Macbeth* (1623)

Watson: "But I have been seated quietly in my chair, and what clues
        can I have given you?"
Holmes: "You do yourself an injustice. The features are given to man as
        means by which he shall express his emotions, and yours are
        faithful servants."
Watson: "Do you mean to say that you read my train of thought from
        my features?"
Holmes: "Your features, and especially your eyes."

DOYLE *The Resident Patient* (1894)

". . . no mortal can keep a secret. If his lips are silent, he chatters his
fingertips; betrayal oozes out of him at every pore."

FREUD *Fragment of a Case History
of Hysteria (1905)*

CLUSTERING AND CONSISTENCY

A single gesture is like a word standing alone. Without a sentence to
give it a context, you can't be sure of its meaning. Clusters of gestures are the
sentences and paragraphs of body language. A puzzled facial expression
shows you only part of what your client is thinking. Does he need more
information? Does what you said contradict something he's heard from
another company? Paying attention to his other nonverbal communication
channels will give you a clearer indication of his feelings. If he is puzzled
and positive, you'll want to act one way. If he is puzzled and negative, your
approach will go in another direction.

Another reason for scanning all channels of nonverbal communication is to look for inconsistencies. As children, we learn to mask our true
feelings with smiles and blank looks. But most of us don't realize that those
feelings are still visible in other parts of our bodies.

Clients may smile while staring into space, turning away from the
seller, playing with objects on their desk, and tapping their feet. They're
bored or uninterested; not happy that you're there. Objections usually elicit
inconsistent responses from salespeople. That smile is still pasted onto their

face, but they'll lean back, cross their legs, avoid eye contact, and pick at their cuticles. They feel rejected and defensive; not glad to answer the client's concerns.

EIGHT BASIC CATEGORIES FOR THE USE OF BODY LANGUAGE IN SELLING SITUATIONS

There are eight basic categories of nonverbal expressions shown on the next few pages. Keep in mind that no single gesture or position means a specific emotion or attitude. However, a number of signals from the same category will clue you in to your client's or your own feelings.

Each category includes an explanation, visual examples, a list of typical body language gestures and positions, and some suggestions for using, or *not* using these signals.

As you read about each of these categories, you'll begin to appreciate the incredible variety of ways people express themselves without *speaking* a word. The categories, with photos, follow on pages 16 to 31.

Category One: Dominance, Superiority, Power

This first category of body language is often exhibited by the company president, or someone who is eyeing the president's position. A person who uses dominance, superiority, and power signals needs to run the show. His attitude may reflect his personality or he may only be playing a role he feels is appropriate for his status. In either case, he will let you, the salesperson, know who is boss—let him. Power signals include:

>   long pause before answering a door knock
>   large desk with owner's chair larger and higher than guest's
>   hands on hips
>   fingers hooked in belt
>   steepling (finger tips touching)
>   hands behind neck
>   leg over chair
>   sitting astride chair
>   exaggerated leaning over table or desk
>   piercing eye contact
>   standing while other is seated
>   palm-down handshake
>   feet on desk

Clients can indicate their need for control by the arrangement of their office furniture and their body language. Don't let them intimidate you, but don't start a power struggle either. Never use these gestures yourself in a sales situation.

Steepling

Hands Behind Head

The Barrier

Category Two: Submission, Apprehension, Nervousness

People who give signals from this second category need reassurance. They are likely to show signs of submission, apprehension, and nervousness if they feel insecure about making decisions. Perhaps they have just been promoted and they don't want to make any mistakes. Try to put them at ease. Observe submission signals such as:

palm-up handshake
hand-wringing
fidgeting
fingers clasped
hands to face, groin, hair
head down
minimum of eye contact
self-beating (rubbing back of neck)
shifting from side to side
briefcase guarding body
constant blinking
throat-clearing
twitching
whistling

Clients who are unsure of themselves and their ability to make good decisions will show their nervousness. Don't mirror their behaviors, or come on too strong. Again, don't use these gestures yourself.

Briefcase Barrier

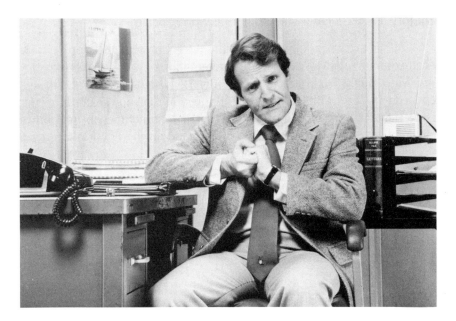

Hand-Wringing

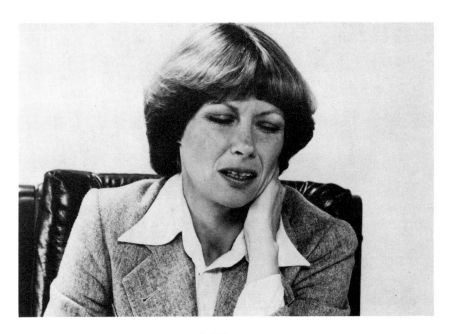

Self-Beating

Category Three: Disagreement, Anger, Skepticism

Category Three signals are usually reactions to what you've said—verbally or nonverbally—during your presentation or while answering objections. Most clients begin indicating their feelings of disagreement, anger, or skepticism in very subtle ways. But, if you don't acknowledge these messages, clients will become increasingly agitated, sometimes to the point of violence. They may even throw things or pound on their desk. Beware of:

      redness of skin
      throw glasses on desk
      fist (in sight, on arm, behind back)
      negative shake of head
      finger-pointing
      pursed lips
      squinting eyes
      thrust-out chin
      crossed arms, legs
      frown
      hands grip edge of desk or table
      turn body away
      finger under the collar

Clients may be hesitant to verbally shout at you, but their body language will warn you that they're unhappy. Don't copy their gestures or stand your ground. Never exhibit any of these extremely negative behaviors during a sales call.

Fist

Pointing

Finger Under Collar

Category Four: Boredom, Disinterest

Messages from the fourth category also reflect the client's reaction to your overall presentation. A sales pitch that works beautifully with one client may seem incredibly dull to another. Your job is to regain the client's attention before disinterest turns to dissatisfaction. Watch for these signs:

dead fish handshake
shuffle papers
clean fingernails
lack of eye contact
look at door, wristwatch, out window, at ceiling
play with objects on desk
pick at clothes
doodle
drum table
tap feet
head in palm of hand
blank stare
pen-clicking
foot-jiggling

Clients may let you give your presentation out of politeness rather than interest. Lots of noise and movement will warn you to stop what you're doing and use some attention-getting tactics. Always look alert to your clients, no matter how bored you are.

Nail-Cleaning

Ceiling-Watching

Fiddling

Category Five: Suspicion, Secretiveness, Dishonesty

The fifth category of nonverbal messages is just as important to salespeople as it is to law enforcement agencies. When a client suspects that you are hiding something or lying, it brings open communication to a halt. And if you feel that your client is being secretive or dishonest, without being consciously aware of your reactions, you're apt to become defensive or angry instead of probing for the cause of his or her behavior. Watch for:

nose-touching while speaking
ear-pulling while speaking
rubbing behind ear while speaking
covering mouth while speaking
consistent avoidance of eye contact
incongruity of gestures
move body away
sideways glance
Granny glance (peer over glasses)
crossed arms and legs with body forward
feet, body pointing toward exit
squint eyes
fingers crossed
smirk (oh really? look)

Clients may distrust your statements or try to hide information they have about your competitors. Remember that almost everyone displays nonverbal cues when lying, so watch your clients and yourself. Avoid making claims that you really don't believe in.

Ear-Pulling

Granny Glance

Nose-Touching

Category Six: Uncertainty, Indecision, Time Stalls

Clients who show signals from Category Six need a break from your presentation. More information is not always helpful when clients can't make up their minds. They will appreciate your sensitivity to their needs when you slow down or pause for a few moments. Note these signs:

pinch bridge of nose with closed eyes
tug at pants while sitting
pacing back and forth
head tilted
fingers to mouth
clean glasses
pipe rituals
bite lip
scratch head
shift eyes to right and left
neck-pulling
tongue to side of mouth
look of concentration while tapping fingers or feet
head down
look of concern or puzzlement

Clients indicate when they need time to think, or they have questions about something which keeps them from making a decision. Give the client some time to gather his thoughts and formulate his questions before probing. If you don't know the answer to a question, say so, instead of looking indecisive.

Pencil to Mouth

Head Down

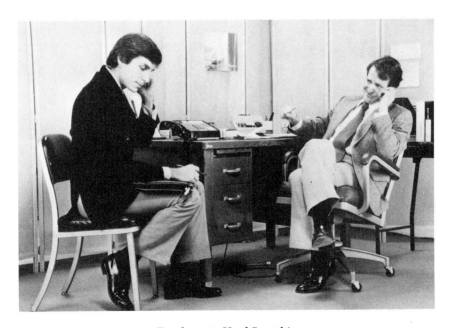

Puzzlement, Head-Scratching

Category Seven: Evaluation

Category Seven signals are important to both you and your client. You need to know that the client is listening to what you're saying. This tells you that you can proceed with your presentation. Your client wants to know you are taking his comments and objections seriously. Look for signs like:

hand gripping chin, index finger up
head tilted slightly
touch tips of temple bars of glasses
nodding
slight blink of eyes
chin-stroking
raised eyebrows and head tilted back
index finger to lips
eye squint
upper-lip-pulling
kicking foot slightly
good eye contact
ear turned toward speaker
glasses (or other objects) in mouth

Clients who are evaluating you or your product will indicate whether they are leaning toward a yes or a no, or simply need more information by their actions. Positive evaluation gestures show your client that you are interested in what he is saying.

Glasses in Mouth

Hand to Chin

Chin-Stroking

Category Eight: Confidence, Honesty, Cooperation

Ideally, everyone should give out Category Eight signals of confidence, honesty, and cooperation. But clients aren't always happy with salespeople and their products. However, you must always exhibit these nonverbal messages. Most clients won't remain aloof for long, if they sense you're sincerely interested in helping them meet their needs. Use selling signals:

palms toward other person, open hands
lean forward in seat
sit far up in chair
good eye contact
legs uncrossed
jacket open
hands to chest
move with speaker's rhythm
free, spontaneous movement of arms, wrists, hands
vertical handshake
back and forth movements of body
feet flat on floor
slight blinking
SMILE

Clients indicate when they are relaxed and happy with your presentation by appearing open and friendly. As a salesperson, you should concentrate on using the body language in this list as often as possible, regardless of your client's negative signals.

Friendly

Smiling

Positive to Negative

THE SIDE-EFFECTS OF LEARNING BODY LANGUAGE

During the first few days of your awareness program in nonverbal communication, you may feel self-conscious and uncomfortable. You will be surprised to notice how many gestures you make, the way you sit, and how often you fiddle with objects or mask your facial expressions in response to a variety of situations. Just remember that most people do not see your body language and will not realize that you are watching theirs. Relax. Enjoy your new knowledge and appreciate the competitive edge you'll have once you move on to the management of these signals.

Another response you may be feeling is worry. You may be asking yourself, "How will I ever be able to concentrate on what I'm saying and what my client is saying if I have to think about all of these other things?"

First, recognize that your unconscious mind is already an expert at body language. You are only training yourself to look for more nonverbal messages. This will make your "impressions" more accurate. At the same time you will be able to modify your own reactions to improve your sales calls.

Second, it helps to know that most people can hear at a rate of 400-500 words per minute, but people speak at a rate of 125-180 words per minute, about three times slower. Instead of becoming distracted during that extra time, you'll be able to use it constructively. You can scan client signals, decide which of the three types of signals (green, yellow, or red) they're sending out, and plan your response.

MOVING ON

Chapter 2 will provide you with a quick method for evaluating nonverbal communication by using the five-channel scan. Knowing which areas of the body to zero in on during a sales call will make reading your client's body language an almost automatic response.

Chapter 3 describes the traffic light model of classifying nonverbal communication. Placing all of your client's messages into one of three clear-cut areas—green, yellow, or red—will further simplify the scanning process.

Chapter 4 deals with the 38 percent of communication not included in nonverbal messages and words—your voice. The impact of your words can be destroyed or greatly enhanced by your use of five areas of vocalization: fillers and sounds, pace, volume, tonality, and emphasis. You are probably more aware of *how* you say things than of your nonverbal communication, so this section will serve as a brush-up course on using speech effectively.

Chapters 5 through 11 discuss specific steps in the sales call. The major nonverbal communication areas to remember are illustrated visually and via the use of sample scenarios.

Your understanding of *Nonverbal Selling Power* will help you overcome buyer resistance, increase sales, and boost profits. Making selling easier and more rewarding is your goal. Getting the most out of every sales call will come naturally when you begin to use 100 percent of your communications power.

CHAPTER 2

The Five Major Channels
of Nonverbal Communication

Monitoring your client's nonverbal signals is not as complicated as it seems. There are only five major nonverbal communication channels: body angle, face, arms, hands, and legs.

A quick scan of these five channels takes only seconds—quite a small amount of time to invest in improving your sales career.

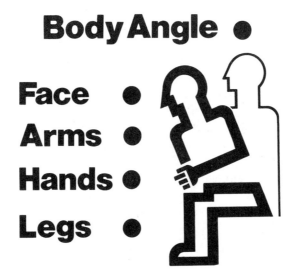

Body Angle ●
Face ●
Arms ●
Hands ●
Legs ●

WHAT TO LOOK FOR IN EACH CHANNEL

You are now aware of the important part nonverbal communication plays in a sales situation. The following section will discuss each of the five nonverbal communication channels in detail to help you focus on key body parts.

Since a client's body language is most reliable when it changes from one gesture or stance to another, we will emphasize movement and intensity. Eyes that stare, unblinking and undirected, say something different than eyes that move from you to your brochures. Legs that are crossed casually and remain still may not be a cause for concern until they are more tightly crossed, or a foot starts to swing, or the crossing is coupled with a shift of the client's body away from you. In any case, it is important to look for a cluster of gestures. A single gesture in one channel doesn't mean anything. That's why it is important to scan all five channels.

A sound knowledge of nonverbal communication will increase your selling power the most when you put it to practical use. Too much information, without an easy-to-use structure, is only confusing. A method for using that information in a sales situation is a profit-making skill. The five-channel scan provides a simple-to-follow technique for doing just that.

CHANNEL ONE—BODY ANGLE

An upright posture or a body movement directed toward you is an important clue signaling that the sale is headed in the right direction. Just as a client will sit closer to you if he feels comfortable and friendly, he will lean his body toward you if he likes what he hears or is intent on listening to your presentation.

When a customer leans back or away from you he is sending a negative message. By using the other channels you will be able to decide whether he is bored or angry, apprehensive or demonstrating superiority.

You should always show interest and a cooperative attitude toward your client by directing your body angle toward him. Back and forth motions indicate drive and a positive outlook. Avoid side to side movements because they suggest insecurity and doubt—remember Dan Rather? Too much motion or complete stillness is likely to project nervousness or tension, so concentrate on using naturally flowing movements. And if you get into a rhythm that matches your clients' speech patterns, they will really feel that you are in step with what they're saying.

Positive Client

Negative Client

Positive Salesperson

Negative Salesperson

CHANNEL TWO—FACE

There is more to a face than a smile. Although a client may hide his disinterest or disagreement behind a grin, his real feelings may be revealed in other ways:

A. **Eye contact**—a customer will avoid eye contact if he is trying to cover up his true emotions, and gaze past you or around the room if he is bored. Increased eye contact signals honesty and interest. Always maintain frequent eye contact with your client.

Lack of Eye Contact   A

B. **Skin color**—a sudden flush or slowly deepening redness of your client's face sends out a vivid warning that something is wrong. Imagine the salesman in the next illustration blushing. Doesn't he appear to be uncomfortable? Without the redness he could simply be scratching his ear. Anger and embarrassment glow like a shiny red apple on some people.

C. **Skin tautness**—tenseness and anger can be detected by looking for signs of tightness around the cheeks, jaw line, and in the neck area. Hold your breath. Now feel the increased tightness in these areas. If you can *consciously* relax your facial and neck muscles when you begin to feel tense in a sales situation, you will *feel* more relaxed.

B   Blushing

C   Tautness

Some smiles are genuine. If the rest of your client's body language tells you that he is open and interested you can be sure that your presentation is hitting the mark.

CHANNEL THREE—ARMS

Where your client puts his arms, how he moves them, and the extent of his movements, will give you further information about his underlying attitude. For this channel, intensity is a key factor.

Here is a progression of arm-crossing movements. Notice how the customer's face and body angle change as her arms become more tightly crossed.

Arms are usually used to provide support for hand movements. Because of this connection, their position can give you advanced warning of hand signals that are likely to follow.

Example 1: Here the client has his upper arms and elbows as far back on the chair as they will go. Before he raised his hands into a "stop" gesture, his forearms were resting on the arms of the chairs, prepared for a defensive movement.

Example 2: This time the client is resting his forearms on the desk, but just barely. He is in a position for a quick retreat or a move closer to you, so you should proceed cautiously.

Example 3: The client who hangs one arm over the back of the chair will tend to lean farther away from you, a negative reaction, or go to a hands-behind-the-head position of dominance. In either case, you do not have his full attention or acceptance.

Example 4: Here the client has his arms well onto the desk as part of his overall body language—he is leaning forward and exhibits interest in your proposal.

A client will use more arm movement when he or she is very involved in conveying an opinion. The broader and more vigorous the gestures, the more emphatic is the client's point. These can be positive, open gestures, or angry threats.

CHANNEL FOUR—HANDS

There are thousands of hand gestures. How can you decide what your client's hands are revealing? By dividing these gestures into three main groups, you will get a general idea of whether the customer is reacting in a positive, cautious, or negative way to your sales call.

1. Open and relaxed hands, especially when the palms are facing you, are a positive selling signal.
2. Self-touching gestures, such as hands on chin, ear, nose, arm, or clothing, indicate tension. Probing for difficulties, or simply relaxing the pace of your presentation may calm the client.
3. Involuntary hand gestures, especially if they contradict a facial expression, indicate the client's true feelings. Watch for tightly clasped hands or fists.

It is very important for you to avoid self-touching and involuntary hand gestures during the sales call. No matter how calm or positive your words are, if the client senses tension or a negative reaction, he will be on his guard and much less receptive to your presentation.

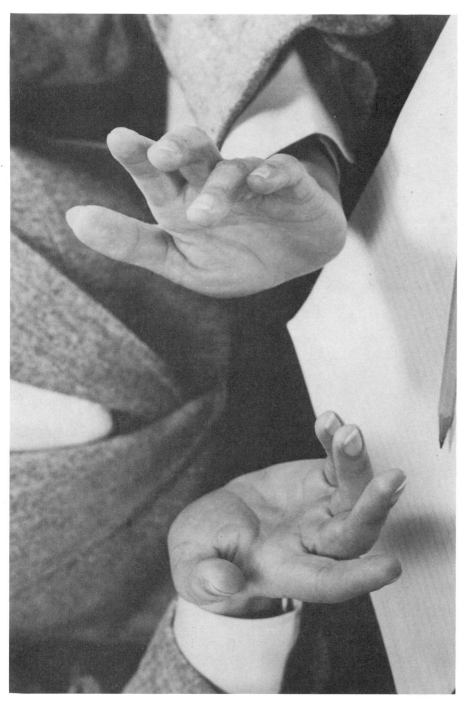

Open hands, palms facing you

Self-Touching

Tightly Clenched Fists

CHANNEL FIVE—LEGS

Most people believe that leg-crossing is done for comfort. Did you ever stop to think about *why* people are comfortable in that position? Usually it's because their bodies are reflecting how they feel inside. A study of 2,000 people by Nierenberg and Calero (*How to Read a Person Like a Book*, 1971) found that *no* sales were made while the participants had their legs crossed. Even if all other channels appear to be open and positive, the customer may have some minor reservations that will prevent you from completing the sale if they are not uncovered and answered.

The following six typical leg positions will show you how this channel of nonverbal communication gets its message across.

1. **Feet on desk**: this position indicates an attitude of ownership and dominance. It is not a posture that will elicit cooperation from the client. Instead, it says "Go ahead and try to sell me."

2. **Figure four**: the average American male crosses his legs by placing one ankle on top of the opposite leg. Although most men
find this position comfortable, it signals that there is something
preventing a completely open mind, when combined with other
closed signals.

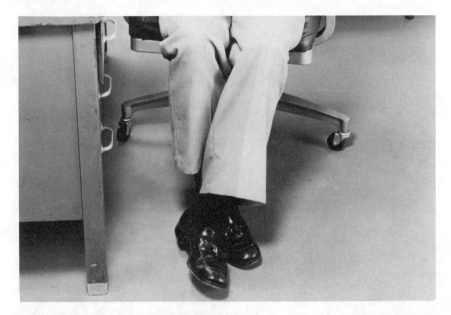

3. **Ankles crossed, feet back:** although your ladies are taught to sit in this position to be properly modest, a client is probably feeling defensive, reserved, or uncooperative when using this leg arrangement, no matter what his or her sex.

4. **Uncrossed, open:** this is the ideal position for both you and your client. It sends a message of cooperation, confidence, and friendly interest in the other person. Use it as much as possible!

5. **Legs crossed away from:** without seeing the other nonverbal channels, you can tell that this sales call is not going well. When legs are in this position, the body is also shifted away from the other person. Always cross your legs toward your client, if you must cross them.

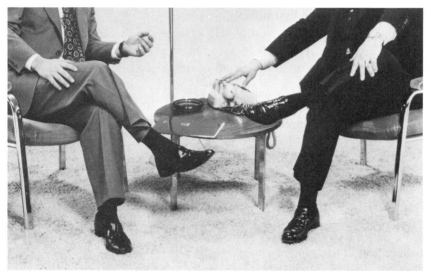

6. **Legs crossed toward:** although it is best not to cross your legs at all, so that your client is encouraged to assume an open posture, this position is acceptable in the early phase of a sale. Mirroring your client's position in this situation may make him or her feel that you are alike and tuned in to each other.

CLUSTERS LINK THE CLUES

In addition to saving time by classifying all body language gestures into a limited number of channels, this shorthand system of reading your buyer's messages reminds you to look for a cluster of gestures. This is important, since many clients are able to control their facial expressions, yet 90 percent of all salespeople tend to judge buyers' attitudes by observing *only* their faces. Some smiles are genuine. If the rest of your client's body language tells you that he is open and interested, you can be sure that your presentation is hitting the mark.

But how many times have you smiled and nodded agreeably to someone you despise? Do you ever frown, even though you're not really that unhappy, just to get your way? Well, clients are people too. Even if they are interested in your product, buyers may frown in an effort to get the price lowered, look puzzled when they want to pump you for information they think you may be leaving out, or smile while thinking about how fast they can get rid of you.

As part of the socialization process, almost all children learn to alter their facial expressions at will. "No one likes someone who looks so grumpy," we're told. "Don't let others know they've made you angry," we're warned. So we develop masks—expressions that project how we should feel, instead of what we're really thinking.

But most people are completely unaware of the secrets the rest of their body is giving away. This is an advantage for the astute salesperson. It is almost as helpful as being able to read minds. All of the information you need is right in front of you. With a little practice, you'll see how easy and profitable it is to turn your new perceptiveness into sales dollars.

DESKS HIDE A MULTITUDE OF SIGNS

Massive desks not only provide the client with a physical barrier, they serve as a visual barrier as well. How do you know if the buyer's legs are crossed, if he's tapping his foot, or cleaning his nails, if you can't see him from the chest down?

For this reason, it is best to choose a chair that is beside the desk, rather than one across from the buyer. In order to see you better, the buyer will turn toward you. This forces him to move away from his desk, exposing all of his nonverbal communication channels.

The following diagrams show the nonverbal signals created by seating arrangements.

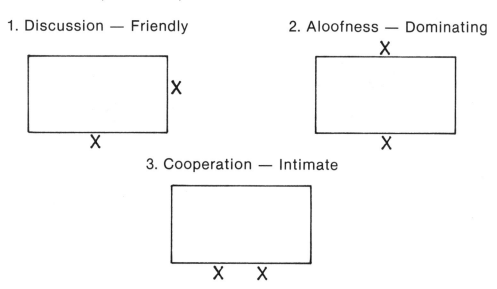

1. Discussion — Friendly

2. Aloofness — Dominating

3. Cooperation — Intimate

In addition to having an open view of your client, as in Diagram 1 above, there is also a more relaxed feeling to the seating arrangement when you are closer to your client. Brochures can be used more effectively because you can maintain control of them and direct the client to the specific areas your presentation emphasizes. If you sit opposite your client (Diagram 2) though, you must stand, read the visual aid upside down, and reach awkwardly across the desk to make your point (see the photo on the next page).

You might sit on the same side of the table as your buyer (Diagram 3) if you are calling on a regular customer and will be seated at a table to discuss plans or specific details on a contract. The most desirable location in any sales situation is wherever you have an unobstructed view of your prospect.

TOO CLOSE FOR COMFORT

Getting close to a client so that you can scan him or her for nonverbal signals can be overdone. If you violate the buyer's "intimate space," usually a distance of up to 1½ feet, you're likely to get only negative readings.

The amount of space a client needs to feel comfortable varies according to a variety of factors. Some of these include cultural differences, age, sex, personality, and the type of relationship you have with him or her. Generally speaking, Eastern Europeans, the French, and Arabs prefer a

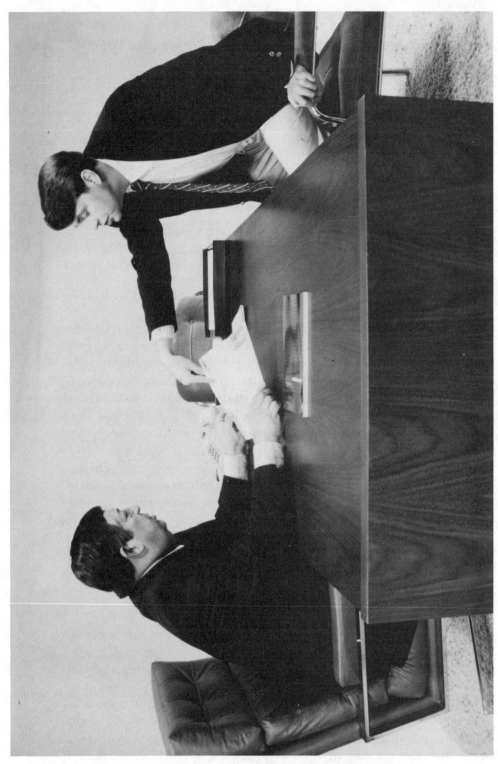

Sitting across from Your Client Creates Problems

much closer distance than the British people do. Peers will tolerate a closer range of contact than people with a wide gap in age. Conversations between females will occur at closer range than male-female talks, and male-to-male encounters show the most distance. People who are outgoing by nature will want to be in a closer, more friendly position than those who are shy or aloof. And if you've been working with a client over a number of years your speaking distance will be less than if you are calling on a client for the first or second time.

Because of these differences, estimates for the amount of space a person will need in a given situation vary. In a client-salesperson situation the following ranges will apply in most cases.

Intimate Space:	Up to 1½ feet. Back off. This is too close for a business situation.
Personal Space:	1-3 feet. Use for longtime clients, and only if *they* are comfortable.
Social Space:	4-7 feet. This distance allows room for stretching and gesturing without invading your client's territory.
Public Space:	10 feet or more. This is a good distance for giving presentations to a group or giving a speech.

CONCLUSION

Your goal in increasing your nonverbal selling power lies in:

- Choosing the appropriate seating arrangement that allows an unobstructed view of the buyer.
- Selecting the appropriate distance—allowing enough space for the buyer to feel comfortable.
- Scanning the buyer's five nonverbal communication channels—body angle, face, arms, hands, legs—so that you can easily decide on the most effective verbal and nonverbal response strategy.

In the next chapter you will discover how to classify the buyer's nonverbal signals in a quick, shorthand manner, allowing you to proceed with confidence from the opening of the sale to the close.

CHAPTER 3

Three Signals for Reading
Your Client Like a
Traffic Light

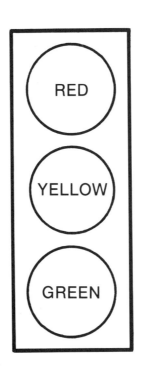

Salespeople who are sensitive to nonverbal cues can read nonverbal signals like a traffic light. Just as the traffic light tells you to go, proceed with caution, or stop, there are body language messages that say the same thing. From your interpretations of the buyer's messages into green, yellow, or red signals, you will know how to proceed with your presentation. By responding appropriately to your client's signals, you will dramatically increase your number of closings and your profits.

How can you tell whether your client is sending green, yellow, or red signals? You use the five-channel scan to look for a cluster of gestures. Basically, a client who is using open, friendly body language in all five channels is sending out green signals. If he or she is exhibiting signs of tension, defensiveness, doubt, or mixes these with friendly messages, you need to proceed with caution when facing such a yellow signal. Increased withdrawal or aggression convey red signals. You will be able to prevent red signals by dealing with the customer's hidden problems before they turn into insurmountable obstacles.

Before going on to the specific strategies for dealing with each type of signal—green, yellow, or red—read over the charts below and look at the sample illustrations. The charts show how the nonverbal expressions for each of the five channels add up to an overall picture of the client's body language.

GREEN SIGNALS

Green signals indicate that your prospect is open and you may move on with your selling strategy.

How You Can Identify Green Signals

Nonverbal Communication Channels	Nonverbal Expressions
BODY ANGLE	Upright or directed toward you
FACE	Friendly, smiling, enthusiastic
ARMS	Relaxed, open
HANDS	Relaxed, open
LEGS	Uncrossed or crossed toward you

GREEN SIGNAL = GO AHEAD

YELLOW SIGNALS

These signals warn you to exercise caution and suggest that an obstacle is preventing open communication with the buyer.

How You Can Identify Yellow Signals

Nonverbal Communication Channels	Nonverbal Expressions
BODY ANGLE	Leaning away from you
FACE	Tense, displeased, skeptical, superior, doubtful, guarded, frustrated, etc.
ARMS	Crossed, tense
HANDS	Clasped, tense, fidgeting with objects or other parts of the body
LEGS	Crossed away from you

Once you have learned to recognize yellow signals, you will probably never again unintentionally push your client into making the next type of gestures.

RED SIGNALS

These signals make it impossible for you to proceed with your selling strategy. You are dealing with nearly insurmountable barriers. The customer is communicating either increased withdrawal or aggressiveness. Red signals tell you that you should stop what you are doing and redirect your approach.

How You Can Identify Red Signals

Nonverbal Communication Channels	Nonverbal Expressions
BODY ANGLE	Leaning far back and away from you, or thrust toward you
FACE	Angry, determined, flushed, tense, tight, head shaking "no"
ARMS	Tightly crossed or thrust out
HANDS	Fists, pointed finger, "stop" sign
LEGS	Tightly crossed away from you or foot stomping

YELLOW SIGNAL = CAUTION

RED SIGNAL = STOP

By the time a client expresses a negative attitude with this much intensity, she has decided that there will be no sale. You may be able to salvage the situation with open, concerned nonverbal signals. But it is far better to deal with her problems early—as soon as you receive the first yellow warning signals.

HOW TO HANDLE GREEN, YELLOW, AND RED SIGNALS

Notice that we did not say 'how to *react* to' these signals. The whole purpose of managing body language is to break away from automatic reactions to negative signals and to respond to them with more useful, positive gestures. The well-known fight or flight reaction to a threatening situation is certainly valuable on a dark city street or if you're on a safari. Clients, however, will not appreciate your aggressive or fearful reaction. They will become more defensive and closed and ultimately show increasingly hostile emotions.

You're no different from the average person if you react in a belligerent or defensive manner to a threat. After all, objections or an outright rejection of a proposal *are* psychological threats—to your prestige, to your self-esteem, to your feelings of confidence. But you don't have to react that way. You have a choice. You can *react* defensively, out of instinct, or you can *respond* with openness, in a thoughtful, professional manner.

Each time your client gives you a signal you have four alternatives. You can ignore the signal, imitate it, synchronize your signals with the client, or try to initiate a different signal. If the client is giving positive signals, your best choice is to synchronize your body language. This gives the customer positive feedback and shows that you are confident about what you are saying. If the client communicates yellow signals, though, you should express green signals while verbally addressing your client's problem.

In order to manage your buyer's signals, you must go through a three-phase strategy called OSL: *observing* your client to gain information; *synchronizing* yourself for a few moments to help your understanding of the buyer's feelings; and *leading* him into a more positive attitude (showing green signals and asking open questions.) Often salespeople use this system in the wrong direction.

Here's an example:

James Pushy is a sales rep for an office supply firm. He arrives for a sales call with a client he has seen only once before. He enters the client's office, shakes her hand and *starts* with: "I'm sure you're going to love the products I've brought to show you today. We're carrying a new grade of paper stock that will make your correspondence look terrific. I also brought . . ."

During the opening, the customer has been showing yellow signals. James has ignored her body messages and unconsciously begun to mirror her negative posture. It is not until his client gets visibly annoyed that James *observes* her red signals and wonders what has gone wrong.

Compare this to the following example:

> Harry Right works for the same office supply firm. He arrives for his sales call and has seen his client only once before. He enters the client's office, shakes his hand, and *observes* that the client seems somewhat preoccupied and reserved (yellow signals). He decides not to begin with his prepared information about his company carrying a new line of top-quality paper stocks. Instead, he asks the client some open questions such as: "I was wondering, how do you rate the quality of the paper you are using now?" or "Could you tell me about some of the experiences you've had using 25 lb. paper stock?" Harry *synchronizes* his own gestures with the client's body language while maintaining an open posture. Harry's open questions, coupled with green signals, will *lead* the prospect to respond with green signals. Harry continues to reinforce his buyer's positive gestures and ends up with a sale.

Your knowledge of the three basic signals (green, yellow, and red) will help you to manage your nonverbal communication as well as your client's. Your own green signals and open questions will lead your client to open up and buy from you.

BEWARE OF LEADING WITH OVERCONFIDENCE

If one sales call is going well, it is easy to slip into an overly confident "I am terrific" state of mind that carries over to the next call. What the next client sees or senses may be a salesperson who is cocky, feels superior to the rest of the world and needs to dominate the situation. Clients will change their signals from green to red with lightning speed if they think that their own needs and interests are not as important as the salesperson's personal goals.

Remember that leadership is always preceeded by followership. Follow the OSL strategy!

The next three sections will explain how to use the traffic light model of reading your client's body language. It is a simple process that will become almost automatic.

COCKY

BODY ANGLE: away from client
FACE: smirking, no eye contact
      with client
ARMS: back against chair
HANDS: one on hip, other
       pointing

DOMINATING

BODY ANGLE: leaning slightly
           back
FACE: raised eyebrows, sideways
      smile
ARMS: back against chair
HANDS: steepling

GREEN SIGNALS: CHOOSE POSITIVE RESPONSES

Always respond to a client's green signals with your own positive gestures. Mutual green signals tend to reinforce each other, making it easier to move the discussion toward a successful close. When a buyer signals green, you know that you can proceed with your presentation.

Look at the examples of green signals below. Notice the positive body language in all the visible nonverbal channels.

CLIENT'S GREEN SIGNALS

BODY ANGLE: slightly forward
FACE: smiling, relaxed, friendly
ARMS: open, relaxed
HANDS: open, relaxed
LEGS: uncrossed, open

MUTUAL GREEN SIGNALS

BODY ANGLE: towards each
                  other
FACES: smiling, relaxed, friendly
ARMS: open, relaxed
HANDS: open, relaxed
LEGS: uncrossed, open

Remember, a client who is not expressing green signals is not receptive to what you're saying. Therefore:

- Never begin a presentation without a green signal from your client;
- Never continue a presentation if your client changes from green to a yellow or red signal;
- Never try to close without your client's green signal.

You may be thinking that you'll never get *any* sales if you use these rules. Luckily, yellow signals can be changed to green ones and green signals into dollars.

YELLOW SIGNALS: ACKNOWLEDGE A CLIENT'S CAUTION

No one likes to be ignored. And that's the message you send if you don't respond in a helpful manner to a client's yellow signals. You must acknowledge the client's doubts or hesitations and put him or her at ease before you can talk persuasively about your product or service. Clients need to feel like individuals. They need to know that you care about what *they* need and want—not what *you* need and want.

TYPICAL YELLOW SIGNALS

DOUBT

BODY ANGLE: hunched over
FACE: furrowed brow, eyes
    squinting, mouth tense
HANDS: fingers or objects to
    mouth

OFFENSIVE

BODY ANGLE: away from you
FACE: tense, frowning
ARMS and LEGS: crossed

No matter what the specific reason behind the yellow signal, your best move is to relax and express green signals, Remember not to mirror or imitate your buyer's yellow signals. This can communicate a negative message that says "Don't buy from me."

POOR SALES REP REACTIONS

RETREAT

BODY ANGLE: away from client
FACE: no eye contact
ARMS: crossed
HANDS: tucked away and covering
       mouth
LEGS: crossed away from client

MIRROR

BODY ANGLE: away from client
FACE: tight, unfriendly
ARMS: tightly crossed
HANDS: tucked into arms
LEGS: turned away from client
      and foot hooked behind
      chair leg

Your best response to a client's yellow signals is for you to express green signals *and* to use open questions to draw out the buyer's real feelings.

Below are examples of open questions that you can use to handle yellow signals:

"I'd like to get your opinion on this . . ."
"How do you see that this will help you in your business?"
"I was wondering . . . how do you see the problem?"
"What do you think about this feature?"
"Would you share your thoughts on this?"
"What do you expect from a product in order to suit your needs?"
"How do you rate the product you are using now?"
"What are your expectations in terms of quality?"

Open questions encourage your prospects to express their concerns about the purchase. Your buyer's answers will give you valuable clues for handling the existing obstacle.

Yellow signals can appear at any time during a sales call. Your client may approach you cautiously at your initial greeting. In this case you need to discover what his or her reservations are. Once you get a green signal and begin your presentation, don't forget to continue scanning. Changes in your client's signals will provide the information you need to continue, slow down, or redirect your approach.

Just as dark clouds forewarn you of an impending storm, yellow signals let you know that an objection is coming. Before your client even thinks about how he'll verbalize his or her objection, you will notice a change in body language. Clients shift farther away from you, facial muscles become tense, their arms cross, they make fists with their hands, or they cross or tighten up their legs.

Avoiding your client's gaze and closing up your body language can begin a spiraling twister of negative signals that ends in bad feelings and no sale. Even when your client seems ready to close, carefully scan his or her nonverbal messages to detect any remaining uncertainties he or she may have—there is an eye to every storm. It can mean the difference between "Where do I sign?" "I'll have to think about it," and "No deal."

Weathering a brief shower is much easier than getting beaten by a hurricane, so watch for yellow signals and deal with them before they develop into more forceful red ones.

RETRIEVE YOUR CLIENT'S TRUST

Failing to respond to yellow signals will push a client into expressing a more intense negative reaction—a red signal. A sharp increase in a buyer's aggressiveness or withdrawal indicates that you have missed his more subtle messages. In the illustrations that follow, you can see that handling the yellow signal in the first picture will get you back into a positive selling situation. By the time she has started to send out red signals, your chances of recovering the sale are much less promising.

YELLOW

BODY ANGLE: straight and tense
FACE: no smile, no eye contact
ARMS: crossed
HANDS: tucked into arms

RED

BODY ANGLE: thrust forward
FACE: angry and tense
ARMS: one close to body, other
       invading salesman's space
HANDS: one pushing down on
       desk, other pointing
       aggressively

In order to salvage this sales call you must:

A. *Express Understanding.* Your prospect must see and hear that you are aware of his or her red signal.

B. *Redirect Your Approach.* Refocus your discussion on the main advantages of your buying proposal.

C. *Express positive nonverbal signals of your own.* Use open, relaxed gestures.

D. *Prevent Red Signals.* Deal with your prospect's yellow signals as they appear.

Scan your prospect's nonverbal communication channels during all phases of the call. Read and respond to your buyer's signals using the principles of verbal and nonverbal selling power.

Catch their yellow signals early so that you can eliminate their doubts and disagreements before they become this serious and cost you the sale.

Don't let your clients get to the point where they look like this (see next page):

HURRY UP!

WHOA!

LISTEN TO ME!

OUT!

SCREENING YOUR RESPONSES

Your own attitude and emotions, expressed via body language, are critical in every sales call.

The following exercises will give you a chance to become aware of usual reactions to negative client signals. This is an opportunity to learn how you can eliminate self-defeating reactions, and how to develop more effective responses.

Although a buyer may not know that you are feeling defensive or angry, due to his lack of conscious perception of your body language, he will sense that something isn't quite right. The bottom line is this—no sale.

Exercise One: Automatic Reactions

When a customer reacts to you or something you've said, you have two choices. You can exhibit an automatic reaction, or you can give a conscious response.

Read the customer expressions in the left hand column and think about your automatic reactions. You can try to visualize the customer expressing the feeling nonverbally, then scan your own body language and describe in one word how *you* feel.

CUSTOMER EXPRESSIONS	YOUR AUTOMATIC REACTIONS
Aggressive	
Analytical	
Anxious	
Angry	
Bored	
Conspiring	
Confused	
Defensive	
Displeased	
Fearful	
Frustrated	
Inattentive	
Nervous	
Puzzled	
Reflective	
Skeptical	
Surprised	
Suspicious	
Superior	

Exercise Two: Negative Salesperson Reactions

Now read over the typical feelings most salespeople experience and translate into negative body language when they *react* automatically to a customer's negative expressions.

Make a note of any of these reactions that apply to you and visualize your customer's body language and your own.

CUSTOMER EXPRESSIONS	NEGATIVE SALESPERSON REACTIONS
Aggressive	worried, tense, angry
Analytical	defensive, skeptical, frustrated
Anxious	enthusiastic, nervous, aggressive
Angry	angry, displeased, inattentive
Bored	bored, forceful, superior
Conspiring	aggressive, anxious, defensive
Confused	fearful, frustrated, aggressive
Defensive	aggressive, displeased, tense
Displeased	angry, forceful, skeptical
Fearful	defensive, frustrated, displeased
Frustrated	aggressive, displeased, angry
Inattentive	tense, suspicious, forceful
Nervous	anxious, displeased, aggressive
Puzzled	angry, anxious, aggressive
Reflective	aggressive, suspicious, tense
Skeptical	anxious, inattentive, superior
Surprised	bored, displeased, puzzled
Suspicious	aggressive, fearful, skeptical
Superior	defensive, angry, worried

Exercise Three: Your Positive Responses

Now that you are aware of your own reactions to negative client expressions, you realize that reacting with your own yellow signals to the client's yellow expressions is a self-defeating proposition.

Next, we can examine the more effective alternative of developing conscious responses—green signals. Think of some positive responses to the customer expressions listed.

CUSTOMER EXPRESSIONS	YOUR POSITIVE RESPONSES
Aggressive	
Analytical	
Anxious	
Angry	
Bored	
Conspiring	
Confused	
Defensive	
Displeased	
Fearful	
Frustrated	
Inattentive	
Nervous	
Puzzled	
Reflective	
Skeptical	
Surprised	
Suspicious	
Superior	

WORKING FROM THE INSIDE OUT

The preceding charts list emotions and attitudes, not specific gestures, for a reason. You cannot hide what you are feeling. Even if you concentrate on keeping your body language open, negative feelings will come through somewhere. Therefore, it is important for you to retrain your mind as well as your body to react in positive, constructive ways to negative buyer signals.

Soon you will see that your knowledge of nonverbal communication is helping you to understand yourself better—all of you. When you notice that you crossed your arms and legs, turned away and slumped in your chair after a client strongly stated an objection, you will understand why you have fallen into that posture. You are feeling defensive and threatened. But you don't have to react that way. You don't have to lose sales. You have the choice not to react but to respond with green signals, thus keeping the lines of communication open with your client. Granted, it is not easy at first, but it is more pleasant and more profitable to respond to objections, or any other negative signals, in a relaxed, calm, understanding manner. After a little practice, your sales calls will become more enjoyable and profitable.

MAKING YOUR GREEN SIGNALS AUTOMATIC

Most of a sales call is spent sitting down. That's why it is worth your time to develop and practice a comfortable sitting position that conveys green signals. Comfort is a matter of habit. Habits can be changed.

If you walk into a room and sit down, what do you automatically do with your body? Scan your five nonverbal channels to check for signals that are detrimental in a sales situation. Do you lean way back in your chair? Are your hands folded tightly, tucked under your arms in fists, or grasping the arms of the chair? Do you cross your legs, tuck them under the chair, stick them way out in front of you, or cross them at the ankles?

As you know by now, these are all positions to avoid during a sales call. Experiment until you find an open, relaxed position that you can use *all the time*. The next step is to constantly be aware of how you sit, every time you sit. Shift into your new comfortable position whenever you fall back into your old habits. With practice, your new position will become your automatic one.

Here is an example of a good green signal position:

BODY ANGLE: slightly forward
FACE: smiling, friendly, good eye contact
ARMS: slightly forward and open
HANDS: open and relaxed
LEGS: open, flat on the floor, one foot slightly in front of the other

NONVERBAL SELLING POWER IN A NUTSHELL

The traffic light model is an easy-to-use tool for putting your non-verbal observations to work for you.

Once you have mastered the five-channel scan and the traffic light model of reading nonverbal signals, observing your own and your client's body language will become automatic. You'll find that using the 55 percent of communication that most people miss—your feelings and attitudes expressed by nonverbal signals—will give you an enormous edge in every sales situation.

"Red"

Your buyer is sending red signals. That means you are facing nearly insurmountable barriers. You've got to stop what you are doing, express understanding and redirect your approach.

"Yellow"

This buyer is sending yellow signals that warn you to exercise caution. Your own words and gestures must be aimed at getting him to open up or he may soon communicate red signals...

"Green"

This buyer is sending green signals that say: everything is "go." With no obstacles to your selling strategy, simply move on to the close.

CHAPTER 4

What You Say
With Your Voice

So far, we've been discussing 55 percent of your own and your client's communications—the nonverbal part. Dr. Mehrabian found that only 7 percent of our emotions and attitudes are expressed in words. That leaves us with another 38 percent to recognize and use—our voices. How you say something is much more important than what you say.

If you listen to motivational tapes, you know that a speaker will inspire you more by his delivery than by the specific words he uses. You probably have a good idea of what Zig Ziglar or Dr. Norman Vincent Peale will say. You buy the tape to hear him say it. Without using any nonverbal signals, these speakers and others express confidence, enthusiasm, and understanding. They convince you of their sincerity and expertise. They know how to use their voices as a tool for creating just the right impression on you.

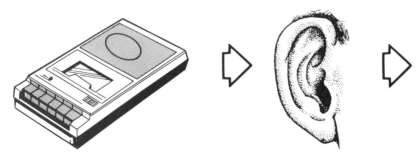

PROVE IT TO YOURSELF

To understand the extent our voices affect the message our words convey, try these three exercises.

1. Praise your dog, or someone else's. Tell him how bright and well behaved he is—but use the loudest, harshest voice you can muster. The dog will probably lower his head or retreat to escape this punishment for something he is now convinced he did to upset you.

2. When your co-workers give you their automatic "Hi. How are you?" line, reply in a cheerful voice "I'm (horrible, ill, nervous, broke, crazy, dead), thank you." Unless you are usually very sarcastic, most people won't notice that you didn't say "fine."

3. During a normal conversation with a friend or spouse, eliminate *all* changes in your voice while you speak—keep the pace, volume, and tone even. Don't even emphasize any individual words. The other person is likely to think you have lapsed into a depressed state, and won't believe anything you've just said.

These are extreme examples of how the way words are spoken can affect the way they are interpreted. Yet they make an important point. Every day, salespeople let orders slip away because their voices don't match what they mean to say. They don't listen to the words *and* the tone of voice a client is using to explain his objections.

By 'tone of voice' we are referring to everything you hear when someone speaks. The five basic components of verbal communication are:

1. Fillers and sounds.
2. Pace.
3. Volume.
4. Tonality.
5. Emphasis.

We will discuss these five verbal communication components in detail. But first, you need to discover what your own voice sounds like. You probably know what it *should* sound like, to fit the role of a professional salesperson. The following tape recording exercises will let you know how it *really* sounds.

PLAYING THE ROLE OF A GOOD SALESPERSON

Actors and actresses are usually asked to just *read* a part at an initial audition. This demonstrates to the director whether the person can verbally interpret what is written into an appropriate characterization. Can they sound like a nervous witness, an overbearing boss, or an Ivy League professor?

Your job as a salesperson requires some of the same abilities. You must be able to sound confident and friendly, concerned and understanding. At the same time you must avoid sounding nervous or uncertain, angry or bored. Fitting into the role of a good salesperson will get you the client's trust and respect.

Before you go on to read about the five verbal communication components we have mentioned, find out how well your voice fits your professional role. First, tape-record yourself giving a presentation you have given before. Second, record your responses to the following client objections:

"Your price is much too high!"

"Why doesn't your product have this special feature that your competition has?"

"Give me three good reasons why I should buy from you now instead of waiting until next year."

"Mr. Brown told me that he bought your service, and he says he spends more time on the phone ironing out problems than he does doing his own work!"

Third, record a casual conversation with a co-worker or friend without your knowing that you are being taped. Ask your partner to start the recording sometime when you are not expecting it.

You may be unpleasantly surprised by what you hear. Do you hear a lot of "uh's" or "you know's" or throat clearings? Doyourwordsallrun together because you speak too quickly or are they   very   slow   but still unclear? Maybe you have to turn the volume up to hear yourself or turn it down to save your ears. Do you sound like yourself? Perhaps your pitch is higher or lower than you thought, or there is a scratchy quality you didn't realize was there, or you speak in a monotone. How do you emphasize your statements? Do you stress words to enhance their importance or do you always stress words at the beginning, middle or end of a sentence, out of habit?

As you can tell from your recordings, there are many ways that your voice influences the impression your words make. Your job as a salesperson depends on producing a good impression. By emphasizing your strengths and eliminating your weaknesses in verbal communication, you'll improve your telephone contacts and enhance your nonverbal communication during sales calls.

COMPONENT ONE: FILLERS AND SOUNDS

Many salespeople are afraid of silence. Even the slightest pause in a conversation makes them uncomfortable. To ease their anxiety, they fill the gaps with non-words, meaningless phrases, and noise, usually without being consciously aware of their poor speech habits.

Below are some common fillers and sounds people use to string words, sentences, even whole paragraphs of dialogue together to eliminate uncomfortable silences.

1. Single syllable sounds: uh, um, ah, eh, oh.
2. Sometimes these are combined with connecting words: and uh, so um, but ah, like eh.
3. A word or group of words that adds nothing to the meaning of the sentence: you know, you see, well so then, ya understand, so really, OK?
4. Hedge words: I guess, maybe, perhaps.

5. Qualifiers: just, that's all, only
6. Noises: throat clearing, sniffling, tongue-clucking, sighs, yawns, coughing, chuckling.

This may seem like a minor problem. But the truth is, many clients will judge your level of confidence and product knowledge by the fluency of your speech. They will interpret fillers and sounds as nervousness or uncertainty. And they are right—to a certain extent. Did you notice that if you heard fillers in your taped speaking samples, they appeared more often during your response to the client objections than during your well-prepared presentation? If they are an ingrained habit, they also appeared in your casual conversation. Your client won't care whether you're using them because of nervousness or habit—he'll simply get a bad impression.

Step One—eliminate fillers. Luckily, these habits are easy to eliminate, but you'll need some help. Ask your family and friends to listen for fillers when you are talking. Have them stop you in mid-sentence every time you use one. This may ruin a few conversations but it will make you keenly aware of how often you rely on these verbal crutches. Soon you'll be stopping yourself before the non-words and sounds are out of your mouth.

Step Two—add silence. Ronald Reagan is a master of the purposeful pause. He knows that it gets the listener's attention and gives the speaker an increased image of credibility. A slight pause between important statements has a wonderful affect on clients as well. They will believe that you are intelligent, analytical, and confident. Another plus is the opportunity you give to your client to make comments and ask questions. Instead of not being able to get "a word in edgewise," the buyer will feel that his opinions are being taken seriously. Customers can be afraid of silence too. They may be compelled to fill up the pauses themselves, thus giving you more information about their interests and concerns. One more advantage to using silence is this: it gives you a chance to listen. You understand more clearly what the client is saying, and can think about what you are going to say in a more relaxed manner if you aren't worried about immediately filling every little pause. Silence is a powerful selling tool. Use it to make a good impression, gain information, and listen to your customer.

COMPONENT TWO: PACE

We are referring to the tempo and rhythm of your speech, not walking the floorboards. The tempo of your delivery—how fast or slow you speak—is another factor in your client's evaluation of you. So is your speech rhythm—flowing or choppy, continuous or in little chunks. In addition to improving your own tempo and rhythm, it is helpful to practice adapting to your client's speech patterns.

Tempo. Speaking speed is a result of your:

- Geographic location and/or birthplace.
- Emotional state.

The scenes below illustrate how these two factors can produce a fast or slow tempo.

1. A saleswoman in a busy New York department store is swamped with customers just before her shift is over.

2. A country grocer in rural Georgia discusses the pros and cons of a new kitchen gadget with a long-time customer.

You can almost hear these people talking because they fit into the following categories.

FASTER	SLOWER
resident of, or born in N.E. United States	resident of, or born in other parts of U.S.
lives or works in city	lives or works in country
busy, overworked, tense	unhurried, enjoys work, calm

As a salesperson, you want to minimize the effect of either extreme. A moderate pace will allow you time to enunciate your words, and will give your client a chance to understand what you are saying without being left in the dust or impatiently waiting for each word. You will gain an extra edge if you can match your speed to your client's speech. This will give him the impression that you are like him, which will put him at ease. In general, then, use a moderate pace most of the time but "when in Rome, do as the Romans do"—speed up or slow down to adapt to your client.

Rhythm. The rhythmic pattern of your speech depends upon your:

- Emotional state.
- Personality type.

SHORT, CHOPPY STATEMENTS	LONG, FLOWING SENTENCES
busy, overworked, tense efficient, scientific, "type A" personality	unhurried, enjoys work, calm easy-going, artistic, "type B" personality

Obviously, most people don't fit completely into one rigid category. But, as a rule of thumb, these descriptions are helpful in analyzing your own rhythmic patterns, as well as your client's.

A dialogue that contains a mix of short, succinct sentences and longer, explanatory statements will give your client the best impression. And, just as you should adapt your speed to your client, you should try to mimic, without being too obvious, your client's speech rhythms. In addition, it is beneficial to nod slightly in time to your client's speech patterns. This gives him the impression that you are following what he is saying and understand his point of view.

Using a moderate tempo and a varied rhythm when speaking will increase your verbal selling power by making your words easier and more interesting to listen to.

COMPONENT THREE: VOLUME

The loudness or softness of your speech is a third factor in your client's evaluation of your professionalism as a salesperson.

Too loud. What do we call a person who is obnoxious, overly aggressive, insensitive, and boorish? *Loud.* Unless your client has a hearing problem, you should tone down an overly enthusiastic, booming voice.

Too soft. People who speak in a barely audible voice seem to be shy, nervous, conciliatory, weak, uncertain or insecure. None of these impressions will help your image as a salesperson.

Aim for a moderate level. If people wince and back away when you speak, tone it down. If they are always asking you to speak up, or repeat what you've said, increase your volume. Keeping your voice at a moderate level or matching your volume to your client is important. A word of warning here—don't match your clients' volume if they get louder due to anger or softer out of uncertainty over a decision. Mirror their volume only when they are speaking in a normal tone of voice.

COMPONENT FOUR: TONALITY

Determining the tonality of your voice involves recognizing its pitch, quality, and range. Your tone should convey a calm, friendly confidence.

Pitch. This is simply the highness or lowness of your voice. Operatic sopranos and small children have high-pitched voices. A chap who sings the bass notes in a barbershop quartet or can do a believable "ho, ho, ho" as Santa Claus has a low-pitched voice. Your normal pitch depends upon your physical make-up and can't be changed (unless, of course, you take drastic steps such as taking hormone shots). But you can control the amount your pitch changes due to emotional factors.

Here are two examples of how pitch can change:

1. Doris is in real estate sales. She generally gets along quite well with clients—until she nears the close of a sale. The excitement of selling a house steadily increases the pitch of Doris's voice. Her clients escape to soothe their headaches. They leave with a vague feeling that Doris is somehow unprofessional.

2. Larry sells wholesale lumber to building contractors. When he becomes angry about something, his voice deepens. This gives it a sinister sound that has scared off several buyers.

These salespeople's voices clued their clients in to their emotional turbulence. No matter how calm they may seem visually, their pitch sends out a warning sign. You can use your knowledge of pitch to better understand your clients if they tend to change pitch when excited or angry.

To improve your own ability to control your pitch, try these exercises:

1. Tell someone about the most exciting thing that has ever happened to you, while preventing your pitch from slowly creeping upwards. Example: "I walked into Mr. Brown's office for a routine sales call and you won't believe what he said. He told me that he really liked my reliable service over the last several years and had managed to increase his budget so that he can buy a whole new telemarketing system for the company—from me."

2. Tell someone about the nastiest thing someone has ever done to you, without letting your pitch drop. Example: "I'd heard that J & P Advertising was ready to switch companies for office machines and paper supplies. So I told Joe (a co-worker) about it over the weekend. That dirty, low-down

sneak went over there on Monday, while I was in a meeting and got the account."

At the end of this section on tonality, you'll see that it's not good to keep the same pitch all the time. This produces a boring monotone. But controlling extreme changes in your pitch will give your clients the impression that you are a stable, reliable person.

Quality. Imagine each of the following people speaking this line: "What did you say?"

a southern belle (1)
a witch (2)
a drill sergeant (3)
a gruff old man (4)
a whining child (5)
a loving spouse (6)

Each of these voices has a distinct character or quality. People are notorious for stereotyping new acquaintances into these types of categories and others. This helps them fit what they hear into a manageable framework. As a salesperson, you want to give your client an accurate impression of your position. To avoid being pegged as someone other than a business-like, yet friendly sales professional, eliminate these unfavorable qualities from your vocal vocabulary during sales calls:

syrupy sweet, placating, submissive (1)
cackling, scratchy, condescending (2)
sharp, domineering, insulting (3)
impatient, cold, nasty (4)
immature, demanding, out of control (5)

Although you don't want to project the feeling of intimacy that you do in speaking to your spouse (6), you can use the same tone quality with clients. You want them to believe that you value what they say and care enough to really understand their point of view.

To improve your tone quality, find someone to imitate. Television, radio, motivational tapes, an exclusive clothing store—these are just a few sources for hearing professionals. Adopt the voice qualities that fit both your personality and your specific sales area.

Range. Everyone knows someone who speaks in a monotone. Whether it's a teacher, boss, friend, or grocery checker, all of their words sound the same. The pace, volume, pitch, and tone stay on one level—and that's boring.

We've been stressing the elimination of extremes in your speech. Here again, you want to keep your client interested in your presentation but you don't want to shock him. A monotone is one extreme. At the other end of the spectrum are the life-of-the-party types. You love to hear them tell stories or describe an unusual experience because they're so expressive. Their pitch jumps from high to low and back again. Their voice quality takes on the characteristics of the various people in the story. You really feel that you are part of their experience.

Such exuberance and animation are great for parties, sports, and talking with kids. But they are too strong for a sales call. An excess of enthusiasm comes across as overly aggressive and pushy in a selling situation. Clients feel much more at ease with someone who speaks in a pleasantly modulating voice—whose words seem to flow in an easy up-and-down motion.

Be particularly conscious of your vocal range in these situations:

1. **Reading lists of features from a brochure.** Read a shopping list out loud. All the items sound the same, don't they? Practice describing each feature as you go along, instead of just spitting them out.

2. **Summarizing special features and client benefits.** This is the time when you will tend to go overboard with enthusiasm. Practice toning down your excitement.

3. **Giving a long presentation.** During this phase of a call you may get into a "range rut" by talking in such a regular up-and-down, up-and-down way that you'll make your client seasick. Remember to vary your range from sentence to sentence.

COMPONENT FIVE: EMPHASIS

A local Virginia radio announcer has such a peculiar way of emphasizing words within a sentence that you lose the entire meaning of her message. Plotting her words on a graph, sentence after sentence follows this pattern:

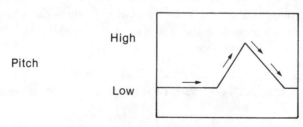

Say the following sentences out loud. Keep your pitch the same until you come to the underlined word—this is where the line goes up on the graph. Each word after this has a slightly lower pitch until you come to the end of the sentence.

"Have a happy hour at the best bar and grill in town."
"Come to the mall's Washington birthday celebration."
"This store has the latest in dresses and sportswear."

The emphasis in these sentences—where the pitch goes up—doesn't really add to the statement. And because you get bored with the pattern, you simply stop listening.

Some people emphasize the first word of every sentence and then trail off. Others, like this announcer, peak at the middle of the sentence. Still others hit their highest pitch at the end of the sentence, after a gradual buildup. There's nothing really "wrong" with any of these speech patterns by themselves. But when they are used over and over again, without regard to the words in the sentence, they do more harm than good.

To get the most out of emphasis, you must increase your pitch on the *most important words* in the phrase. Some sentences may have three or four peaks. Lead-in sentences may not have any sharply emphasized words at all.

Here is a familiar sales pitch from a television commercial. Notice how the peaks (the underlined words) focus your attention on the main points of the sentence.

"Four out of five doctors recommend new Extra Strength Zappo pain reliever.

You can use emphasis in the same way to help your clients hear the key words in your statements. Let's say that you are selling a computer system to a small businessman who feels threatened by complicated machines. Although you will want to mention the system's capabilities—memory, compatability with other systems, types of software available—you can keep these features less confusing by not heavily emphasizing any of them. What you want to emphasize, because it's what the customer wants to hear, is how easy the system is to use. For instance:

"One of the reasons other businessmen like yourself have purchased this model is because of its easy-to-follow directions. This computer is what we call user friendly. It is designed to function for people who have little or no computer background. In addition, we offer a toll-free number to call 24 hours a day, so that we can help you with any questions you may have right away."

Most people are not very good listeners. They pick up the meaning of what you say by latching on to words that stand out. Make sure that you emphasize the words that are most important to your statements so that they get the right message.

If you don't believe that emphasis can make much of a difference in the meaning of a sentence, hear how the interpretation of the sentence below changes when each of the words is stressed.

"Did you go with him?" (a simple yes or no)
"Did you go with him?" (you as opposed to others)
"Did you go with him?" (perhaps you said you wouldn't)
"Did you go with him?" (or by yourself or with others)
"Did you go with him?" (reflecting envy, disdain, shock)

RETEST YOURSELF

After reading this chapter and trying out the suggested exercises, retape yourself in the situations you recorded earlier. (p. 83-84). Do you hear any differences? Even if you haven't had much time to improve your speech, you will notice more details of your voice than you did before.

Awareness is the key to making the most of your verbal communications. Opening your ears so that you hear the 38 percent of attitudes and emotions expressed by "tone of voice" will give you another selling edge. You'll easily outperform the salespeople who are not using this 38 percent to their advantage.

PART II

Using Nonverbal Selling Power During Every Phase of the Sale

CHAPTER 5

Preparation

To many salespeople, call preparation means to scratch a few notes on the back of an envelope, review the sales literature, and hope for the best. Yet a more thorough process of thinking ahead will eliminate many problems before they ever arise.

TAKING THE TENSION OUT OF SELLING

There is one major reaction to a sales call that you can prepare for in advance so that you are at your best during the actual call—STRESS. When high dollar figures and personal prestige are at stake, you naturally feel pressured. Often, the physical symptoms caused by stress handicap you enormously. You can lose the sale before you ever get to a formal presentation. Your nervousness and tension make the client feel uncomfortable and a spiral of yellow to red signals begins.

The photo on the next page illustrates some of the typical physical symptoms of stress.

You may be the type who hides your nervousness very well, but feels all knotted up inside. Or you may not experience any internal symptoms, but your hands shake or twitch. No matter how you react to stress, it is important that you prepare for it before the sales call begins.

First, try some simple relaxation techniques. A few minutes of quiet time to relax your shoulder muscles and gain control over your breathing

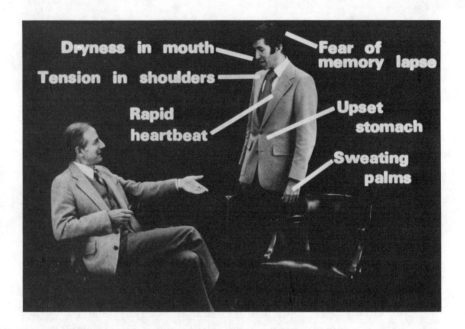

rate will help to reduce your tension. When your body is in an open, relaxed position, it has a positive psychological effect. You start to believe that you are calmer.

CREATIVE IMAGERY

Another step you can take, one which will strengthen your inner confidence, is a technique called creative imagery. Basically, you use your imagination to visualize what could happen during the call—the worst possible client reactions, and then the best. This gives you the opportunity to screen your own reactions in these situations.

Exercise One. Using the top photo on page 97, make a list of your 'worst' customer reactions. Perhaps you've recently encountered a particularly difficult client, or there is a specific objection that really bothers you.

Now that you have a clear image of what your negative client looks like, and what you'll hear him say, think about the five-channel scan.

Now hear the customer saying:

"What do you MEAN there'll be a two-week delay in delivery?"

Finally, think of your positive verbal and nonverbal responses.

Worst Reaction

Exercise Two. The client (below) shows all the classic green signals. Review the five channels and hear the client say:

"I've heard a lot about this new product of yours."

Best Reaction

Now, imagine your own verbal and nonverbal responses.

Most salespeople assume that they know how to handle these positive signals. But there are a few key points to remember so that you are prepared to make the most of green signals.

- Be flexible—be prepared to shorten or lengthen your presentation to keep the client interested.
- Temper your enthusiasm—remain controlled and friendly so that you don't come on too strong.
- Continue to scan—detecting yellow signals as soon as possible is your best approach for a successful sales call.

The entire process of creative imagery takes only a few minutes. By anticipating the *worst* possible client reaction, you assure yourself of your ability to handle anything. By preparing for the *best* possible client reaction you:

1. Put yourself into a confident frame of mind.
2. Make sure that you don't get carried away in the excitement of the moment and lose a perfect opportunity for closing a sale.

THE SINCERE SMILE

The very first thing your client will notice when you walk into his office is your face, particularly your smile. Customers can easily distinguish between a "phony" smile and a sincere smile. The sincere smile flashes repeatedly and appears at appropriate times. The "phony" smile fades quickly and is used to cover internal anxiety or hostility. In other words, if you're nervous, the client will notice.

We've found a practice exercise that is easy to use, so that you can train yourself to always use a sincere smile: put on a smile, hold it for 21 seconds. Now watch how your mood changes. At first you may feel odd about this. Next you may feel like smiling at yourself. By the time you reach 21 seconds, you are ready to smile sincerely.

James Laird, a psychologist at Clark University in Worcester, Massachusetts, has found that a smile can trigger memories as well as a good mood. When students were asked to describe memories of neutral words like "car," what they said depended upon whether they were told to smile or frown while talking. Smiles helped recall pleasant memories, and frowns triggered unpleasant ones.

You can use this same method when preparing for a sales call. Smile while you think about each step of your meeting with a client—opening, needs analysis, presentation, handling objections, and closing. This will help you to recall the times that you succeeded in getting through a sales call all the way to a prosperous close.

MAKING A GOOD IMPRESSION

Preparing for a sales call is not limited to thinking about the coming meeting while you're waiting in the client's office. Just as you can practice your smile well before the call, you need to consider the type of visual impression you will make on your client.

We're taught that appearances shouldn't determine our reactions to people—it's what's inside that counts. But your customer's primary aim is not to become friends. A client needs to decide, in a short amount of time, whether you are reliable, truthful, and professional. Even before you verbally greet a client, your dress, posture, and bearing indicate how you feel about your job. So here are a few tips for creating a positive first impression that can make what you say—with your words, your tone of voice, and your body language—much more effective.

1. **Dress conservatively:** Each area of sales has a uniform, from Wall Street pin-stripe to Record Store Khakis and sports coat. Outlandish fashions may catch the client's attention, but they'll leave a *negative* impression.

2. **Colors create an image:** Solid suits of gray, beige, and navy blue, with blue shirts for men, and two-piece dresses with a jacket or a suit in similar colors for women are basics. You should avoid aggressive colors of orange or turquoise, and any color that doesn't suit your hair, eye, and skin color. To determine your best colors, you can get a "color draping" by a professional image or color consultant.

3. **Neatness counts:** Attention to the details of your clothing, such as a well-pressed shirt and polished shoes, tell the customer that you're conscientious. A disheveled appearance gives the impression of disorganization and carelessness.

4. **Quality is the key:** No matter what the price of your suit or dress, get a good tailoring job, and never skimp on accessories. Ties, jewelry, and attaché cases that are tacky can ruin your overall image.

5. **Stand tall:** Good posture and a confident stride say you are happy and capable. Slouching, or a shuffling gait can convey an "I don't care

about what I'm doing" attitude, and will make a well-tailored outfit hang poorly.

When you realize that the deciding factor for a sale could rest on your client's visual impression of you, doesn't it make sense to project the very best image possible? A basic, conservative wardrobe, attention to the details of your appearance, and a confident stance will increase your self-confidence and provide an excellent foundation for your body language skills.

PREPARING FOR THE CLIENT WHO IS "DIFFERENT"

By "different," we mean unlike yourself. It's inevitable that you'll encounter clients whose wealth, education, race, culture, sex, or age are unlike your own. Feeling uncomfortable will put you at a severe disadvantage. In fact, your client is likely to assume the worst from your tension—that you're stupid, or a bigot, a chauvinist/feminist, or too young/old to know what you're talking about. Invest a few minutes to think through your approach and responses to those who are "different" from you. You'll be more relaxed, and better prepared to avoid communicating any negative emotions you may have.

Differences in Wealth and Education

Many salespeople tend to express signs of tension when dealing with a "richer" or "better-educated" prospect. This tension can lead either to a high-pressured sales presentation or increased confusion and loss of confidence.

It may help to keep in mind that the purpose of the call is not to measure the differences between the client and yourself, but to get the order. Check your own tension level during the call. Remember that the relaxed salesperson is always perceived as superior.

Differences in Race and Culture

The color of the skin is communicated nonverbally. Culture is communicated through tone of voice (foreign accents). Beware of your own negative feelings and attitudes about blacks, whites, and foreigners. Try harder to understand the differences and to bridge the gaps.

Studies have shown that black people have greater "reading skills" in the field of nonverbal communication. However, many black people tend to express tension signals and decreased eye contact during selling situations with white people. People from Latin America tend to have less frequent eye contact when dealing with the Non-Latino client.

How can you bridge the gap? Rehearse increased eye contact. Use relaxation techniques prior to the call. Visualize. (The charisma of Sidney Poitier lies in slower movements and increased eye contact!) If you are white and calling on a black prospect, use open and relaxed postures. Observe all five communication channels. Try to accept and understand any differences and then focus on your selling task.

Differences in Sex

In male/female selling situations, it is advisable to avoid communicating nonverbal expressions that hint at seduction or aggressiveness.

The professional salesperson has to make a clear commitment to the initial task, while maintaining a friendly relationship.

Women should avoid "preening" gestures (e.g. arranging hair, palms facing male). Men should avoid aggressive postures such as hands on hips, moving too close, staring at breasts, etc.

Use creative imagery prior to the call. Become aware of any negative fantasies or distracting thoughts and anxieties about the call. Try to assume a firm and friendly attitude. The key to success is to balance these qualities. If you are too firm, you'll meet resistance and won't reach your goal. If you are too friendly, you pursue the wrong goals for a selling situation.

Differences in Age

Did you know that your chances for making a sale decrease proportionally to the age difference between you and your prospect? An age difference of more than 10 years can create an increasing number of tension signals (expressed by the younger person)—and withdrawal signals (expressed by the older person). To minimize difficulties due to an age difference, try the following strategies for "tuning in" to your client.

To bridge the generation gap, "tune down" to an older client. This means that you will show increasingly relaxed postures and movements, as well as poised behavior. Avoid mirroring the older client's posture. Don't switch quickly from slow to fast movements. Imagine how you would act, feel and think at your prospect's age by visualizing yourself 10, 20, or 30 years older.

Bridging the generation gap in the other direction requires you to "tune up" to a younger client. Show increased enthusiasm, mental readiness and flexibility. But don't get too excited. Try to be complimentary. Imagine how you acted, felt, and thought at the younger prospect's age.

PEOPLE LIKE PEOPLE LIKE THEMSELVES

You can't possibly be like everyone else. But you minimize your differences by:

1. Recognizing your unproductive reactions to people who are unlike yourself.

2. Practicing responses that will lessen your differences.

When you go on a sales call, you are selling to an individual—not just a company, or a purchasing agent. Individual consideration of that person's status (wealth and education), race, culture, sex, or age will greatly improve your chances for a successful close. Knowing how to respond before you are face to face with "different" clients is part of a thorough preparation program.

PROCRASTINATION

How many times have you put the same unpleasant task on a list of "do today" jobs, and never quite gotten around to it?

For example, you may have meant to call a difficult prospect for several days. Every day it's on your list of things to do and every day it gets postponed. Or you thought you'd turn in your expense report on Monday and it's already Wednesday.

Preparation is useless if you don't follow through. Putting off a task may relieve you of a short-term discomfort, but it turns the job into a long-term frustration. You continually remind yourself that you should have made that call and it ruins your relaxation time. Or you can't remember what you spent because it's been so long since you spent it.

Here's an anti-procrastination exercise that will help you deal with tasks you've been putting off.

1. Develop a list of tasks for each business day.

2. At the end of the day, write next to the tasks you didn't complete:

a. The negative thoughts you had about these tasks during the day.

b. Worries and anxieties you have experienced which are related to these tasks.

Example of an unfinished task and the writing process:
"Call Kaiser Enterprises today."

a. "I don't think they will be able to afford our high price."

b. "I am afraid they will say no."

At this point you should reappraise your negative and unrealistic thoughts and give yourself some useful suggestions. Using the above example, you could write down these responses:

a. "That's unrealistic! How do I know what they think? I need to stop mind reading."

b. "So what! That doesn't mean the end of the world. I'll create an opportunity to learn more about their true needs."

Once you've eliminated your irrational thoughts, you've eliminated your reasons for procrastinating. Procrastination hurts less than failing, but it hurts all the time. It interferes with your life and affects your performance. What's worse, it doesn't protect you from failing. The little procrastination barriers that you build inside yourself become giant roadblocks to the pursuit of your goals.

HOW YOU FEEL ABOUT YOURSELF IS WHAT THE CLIENT SEES

A temporary case of nerves, or an occasional off-day can usually be turned around by the conscious use of positive nonverbal communication—green signals. But a more serious problem with stress, a poor self-image, or continuing difficulties dealing with people who are "different" from you will really hurt your sales. Even the best-planned nonverbal signals will appear inconsistent to the client. Prepare for stress, a professional appearance, and difficult clients before the call. Then remember that in public you must always—

USE AN EFFECTIVE WAITING POSTURE

Before you see your client, you will probably have to wait in a lobby, a reception room, or an assistant's office. Many of the preparation exercises we have suggested can be briefly reviewed at this time. But you must take care to monitor your nonverbal behavior while you're deep in thought, because office insiders are sure to notice you while you're in their territory. An efficient, observant secretary will notice your waiting posture and make a mental note of it—either positive or negative.

For this reason, it is important for you to sit in the comfortable green signal posture we asked you to develop in Chapter 3. As you sit down, take a quick five-channel scan of yourself. Make sure that you aren't reinforcing your feelings of tension by using negative body language. Then:

- Relax.
- Use creative imagery.
- Check over your appearance.
- Resist visualizing your client as "just like you." Be prepared to bridge the differences between you and your client.
- Remind yourself that maximum flexibility will translate into maximum potential.
- SMILE!

CHAPTER 6

Opening

The opening phase of a sales call begins the moment you enter your client's office. If you are well-prepared and have used the suggestions for waiting room relaxation, you are already exhibiting green signals.

EXPRESSING CONFIDENCE WHILE STANDING

As you stand in front of your client to greet him or her, avoid the two biggest mistakes salespeople usually make:

1. Communicating nonverbal expressions of insecurity by moving their bodies from side to side.

2. Communicating aggressiveness by putting both hands on their hips, standing directly opposite the client.

To appear confident, instead of insecure or aggressive, try these tips:

- Keep feet one foot apart—this gives you more stability than having them spread only a few inches apart and will help you avoid swaying from side to side. (70 percent of your body weight is above your hips!)
- stand at a 45° to 90° angle, instead of straight across from your prospect—this seems less threatening.
- Keep your arms and shoulders relaxed and off your hips.

- Stand in the "personal" zone of 1½ to 4 feet—too close is threatening and too far is impersonal.
- Remember to keep your briefcase at your side, not directly in front of you as a barrier.

Poor Stance

Good Stance

THE FRIENDLY HANDSHAKE

A firm, well-timed handshake can get your meeting off to a good start. We suggest that you stop just out of reach of your clients so that they must approach you for this initial contact. This gives you a psychological advantage of control over the situation while not being blatantly aggressive. Female clients will expect a welcoming handshake. Failure to do so will give them the impression that you don't respect their position in the company and will trigger yellow signals almost immediately.

Use the following guidelines to achieve a friendly handshake and access to your client's attitudes and emotions early in your opening.

1. Keep your hand in a vertical (straight up and down) position—palm down can communicate domination; palm up can communicate submission.

2. Apply moderate pressure—overly forceful handshakes (bone-crushers) convey aggression and a lack of consideration; limp handshakes (dead fish) convey insecurity, or lack of interest.

3. Move your arm at a moderate pace—quick, jerky, overly enthusiastic hand-pumping sends all but the most familiar clients into retreat; no movement at all shows a lack of energy and cooperativeness.

4. Pay attention to how your client returns your handshake—all of these interpretations apply to clients too!

The Solid Vertical Handshake

SELECTING A SEAT

Your next move will be to choose a seat. Remember, the best arrangements are either at a small table in similar chairs, or to the side of your client's desk. This is because:

- You have a clearer view of all five of your client's nonverbal communication channels.
- It creates a friendlier, less formal, and more cooperative atmosphere than sitting across from your client with his or her desk as a barrier.
- You are better able to show your client brochures and other visuals without getting into awkward postures, having to read upside down, or losing control of them. (When your client has the brochure, he can look at it, play with it, and become distracted by it; if you have the brochure, you can take it back when you want to go on to other points in your presentation.)

STATING THE PURPOSE OF YOUR CALL

Your client's time is a precious commodity. Using it carelessly is one of the fastest ways to lose a sale. To show your clients that you appreciate the time they spend with you, it is important to state the purpose of your call right away. Customers need to know that they are making a good investment by taking time to hear your presentation. The best way to assure them of this is to give them the promise of a benefit. For instance:

"The reason for my call is to help you with your (production, organization, information retrieval, etc.) needs."

"I'd like to show you a way to increase your productivity by 25 percent."

"In just (7, 9, 11) minutes I can explain our new (specific product, service) and describe how it can save you money." (Odd numbers have more impact than even ones.)

By giving prospects a reason for investing their time, you focus their attention on your product or service. This eliminates the silent guessing game clients play when you don't state your purpose early, and distinctly. Instead of listening to you, they may be asking themselves:

"What is this salesperson really trying to sell me?"

"I already have a contract for this (product, service), so why should I waste my time listening to this presentation?"

"How long is this thing going to take?"

Sometimes, you can make a better impression by postponing the call to another day. Clients who are pressured for time won't be receptive to anything you say. Maybe they're under a tight deadline, or they're just having a bad day. If you have been communicating green signals, and your client is still flashing yellow or red signals after your positive opening statements, it's probably a problem unrelated to you. Suggest an alternate time for your presentation and reinforce your benefits statement:

"If it is inconvenient for us to discuss this important matter of (product, service) today, I'd be glad to come back (this Thursday, next Monday—be specific) when we'll have more time to talk about improving your productivity (restate benefit)."

Another possible reason for an unfriendly reception is a client's negative feelings about your company or a particular product or service you're offering. This problem should be dealt with early in the call by using benefit statements about your satisfied clients, and citing proofs of the reliability of your company. Use these questions to probe for any impressions or knowledge your client has about your company.

"MZQ Corporation and BYX Enterprises have been very pleased with our line of products. PAUSE. They even put this in writing." SMILE.

If clients have heard poor reports they are likely to say so at this point. Address their problems to eliminate their yellow signals.

"According to a recent article in this trade journal, we had the highest reorder rate (number of renewed contracts, best safety record) during the past twelve months." PAUSE. (Have your documents ready.)

Again, if clients have read information that contradicts this statement, they will take this opportunity to express their concerns.

Remember that open questions and your own green signals are designed to get your client to "open up."

"I'd like to get your objective opinion. How would you rate our products and services?" SMILE, PAUSE, and LISTEN.

(Customers who have never heard of your company need to be approached differently.)

As you receive the customer's answers, continue by thanking him or her for sharing this information with you.

Client reservations that are not brought out and dealt with during the opening phase will:

- Distract your client from your presentation.
- Prevent your client from weighing your statements objectively.
- Increase your client's feelings of hostility or impatience because your call seems like a waste of time.

If you work for a small company, a new company, or a firm that has just changed its name, you will have to work harder at coming up with a winning opening statement. Name-recognition plays an important part in sales. Clients feel safe with well-known companies and tend to give the advantage to representatives of established firms. You can establish the same feeling of safety by using verbal and nonverbal selling power to develop trust. Whenever you can, list the benefits of your company's product or service over your big-name competitors:

> "Our product (state brand name) has all the same features (use open palm gesture indicating honesty) as the leading competitors have (avoid stating any competitor's name), but because our overhead expenses are lower (use firm eye contact), we can offer it at a better price (smile, nod head)."

> "Certainly, some of our competitors have a very large service department, but (state company name—use eye contact) can offer faster (pause), more individualized (tone of voice emphasis) attention because we are (open palms gesture, raise eyebrows slightly) a local firm."

Prospects want you to reassure them that they will get the most for their money and the best possible quality. Explain that you understand how a poor or defective product will waste their time and money, and can even be bad for their careers because wrong decisions are remembered by their bosses. Convince your clients that your are offering more quality as well as higher value and you'll establish trust and green signals throughout the call.

REASSURING THE NERVOUS CUSTOMER

Your relaxed and open postures will do wonders in reducing your prospect's initial apprehension. Some clients are harder to "open up" than others, though. They may feel insecure or frustrated; they may be bored or overworked in their jobs. These feelings can show up as disinterest, hostility, or simply "nervousness." Some helpful hints for relaxing this type of client can be gained from one profession that must constantly sell "unwanted" services—dentistry.

Dentists and their staffs are aware of the anxiety their services produce. They also realize that those who say they're not nervous may be the most jittery patrons. So they look for "displacement gestures." Tapping fingers, flipping through magazines aimlessly, fiddling with objects, and chain-smoking all indicate nervous energy. To calm their patients, dentists know that they need to reassure them through pleasant music, calm, low-key conversation and light humor. The main goal is to assure the patients, through their own actions, that everything is fine.

In selling, you may notice similar displacement gestures. To help calm such a prospect remember to:

1. Avoid "mirroring" the client's nonverbal gestures or movements. Resist the subtle, unconscious urge to respond to these gestures by scratching your head, fiddling with a match, jiggling coins in your pocket or by shifting your posture too often.

2. Lead the client to imitate your own expressions of confidence and reassurance. Communicate relaxed gestures and postures, maintain a comfortable distance between yourself and your client (4-5 feet), and consciously lower your shoulders (raised ones indicate tension), tilt your head slightly (showing interest) and slightly close your eyelids (wide-open eyes signal fear).

A SAMPLE OPENING

In the following opening scene of a sales call, note the salesman's verbal and nonverbal selling techniques and identify as many inappropriate and self-defeating moves as you can on a separate sheet of paper.

Tom Lane, a computer salesman for a small company, is calling on Joe Smith for the first time. Tom is tense because he has heard that Joe is shopping around for a new system and has talked to salespeople from some of the most prestigious companies.

After waiting for 16 minutes, Tom is led into Joe's office. Joe is seated behind a large desk. (Note: the numbers indicate nonverbal signals which will be evaluated and explained at the end of each scene. All scenes are illustrated with action photos.)

THE SCENE

Tom (1): (immediately walks up to Joe's desk, reaches across the desk and extends his hand.)
"Hi, I'm Tom Lane! How's everything today?"

Joe (2): (leans back slightly, shakes Tom's hand with one quick downward motion and lets go, motions to a chair across from him.)

"Fine, thank you, Mr. Lane. Won't you have a seat?"

(said in a monotone.)

Tom (3): (takes chair indicated by Joe although there is a chair to the side of the desk; sits far back in the chair, puts briefcase in his lap; smiles but is very tense.)

"I understand you're interested in upgrading or replacing your computer system. Is that correct?"

(pauses briefly but goes on without getting an answer.)

"My company, JD Computers, can provide you with a system that will cover all of your present needs, and can be easily expanded as necessary."

(hands a brochure to Joe from his briefcase; briefcase remains in his lap)

Joe (4): (takes brochure, flips through it with one hand while tapping on the desk with the other. Joe is leaning back and isn't smiling.)

Joe says nothing.

Tom (5): (leans farther back in chair, taps fingers on chair; Joe continues his silence so Tom puts briefcase down, leans forward, crosses one arm, points with finger to brochure.)

"As you can see on the third page, our system is compatible with your present one, so you wouldn't need to replace all of your equipment at one time."

(Tom's voice quivers slightly, he shifts and fidgets in his chair—he would like to go around to Joe's side of the desk to point out specific features but is afraid of being rebuffed; he avoids eye contact.)

"Do you have any specific questions I could answer for you?"

Joe (6): (pushes the brochure back across the desk to Tom, frowns, and crosses his arms tightly.)

"Not really."

Tom (7): (takes back the brochure, plays with it while speaking.)

"Well, I'd like to ask you some . . ."

Joe (8): (hands go up in a stop gesture.)

"I'm sorry, I'm running late today. I'll keep the brochure on file and call you when we get close to a decision."

At this point there is no way for Tom to salvage this sales call. Tom did much worse than most salespeople do during any single sales call, but every time you show yellow signals, or fail to acknowledge your client's yellow signals, you are jeopardizing your chances for a successful close.

Here are the mistakes Tom made, and the client signals he missed:

(1) Tom did not stop before reaching the desk to give Joe the opportunity to rise, come around the desk, and shake hands. Extending his arm across the desk puts Tom in an awkward position and gives the impression of invading the client's territory. Tom is overly exuberant in his greeting.

(2) Joe shows his disinterest in the sales call by leaning back, using a minimal handshake, and using a very formal greeting said in a monotone.

(3) Tom ignores Joe's formal manner of addressing him and takes a seat across from Joe (a chair at the side of the desk was farther away from Tom's standing position so he sat in the first available seat. Tom immediately sends out yellow signals by sitting back, using the briefcase as a barrier, and showing facial tension. Tom asks a closed question and fails to wait for an answer. Then he uses his visuals too early, handing them over to Joe instead of using them to point out particular points.

(4) Joe is distracted by the brochure and it provides him with something to use for his displacement gestures. He is signaling yellow by leaning back and not even trying to smile. His lack of comments reinforces his lack of interest in Tom's call so far.

(5) Tom is at a definite disadvantage without control of his materials. He has some good points to make but is drowning them in his negative body language. Tom begins to mirror Joe's yellow signals by leaning back in his chair and tapping his fingers. He then moves forward with a closed and aggressive posture. His lack of eye contact also signals yellow.

(6) Joe's signals are moving from yellow to red as he crosses his arms tightly, pushes the brochure away, and frowns. His continued lack of comments about Tom's product is a sure sign that Tom has already lost him.

(7) Tom now shows displacement gestures by fiddling with the brochure. Instead of trying to get the customer to open up, he again uses a closed question.

(8) There is no mistaking Joe's red signals now. He will say anything to get rid of Tom at this point. Tom has no choice but to leave as graciously as possible.

Even though Tom had some good verbal points to make, he lost the sale because of his lack of nonverbal selling power.

Reading nonverbal communication signals requires ongoing observation and awareness. Here is the sequence of photos that illustrate what Tom should have noticed as he spoke with Joe:

**Joe's Nonverbal
Signals**

BODY ANGLE: straight
FACE: serious, eyes
       partially closed
ARMS: back in chair
HANDS: folded

1.

Tom: "I understand you're interested
    in upgrading or replacing your
    computer system."

BODY ANGLE: straight
FACE: displeased
ARMS: back in chair
HANDS: fiddling

2.

Tom: ". . . our system is compatible
    with your present one."

BODY ANGLE: straight
FACE: displeased
ARMS: back in chair, one
      raised
HANDS: one up for caution,
       other grasping
       brochure

3.

Tom: "Do you have any specific questions
I could answer for you?"

BODY ANGLE: leaning back
            and away
FACE: angry
ARMS: back against chair

4.

Joe: "I'm sorry, I'm running late today.
I'll keep the brochure on file."

JOE REVISITED

You've seen what can happen when a salesperson like Tom sends out yellow signals and fails to respond to a client's yellow and red signals.

Now, let's follow Tom after he has learned to monitor his own and his client's signals. This time, think about what Tom did well and why.

Tom is working for the same firm. He's calling on Henry West for the first time. Tom is certain that he can offer Henry a better price and more dependable service for his product than his larger competitor.

THE SCENE

Tom (1): (walks toward Henry's desk, slows while greeting Henry.)
"Hello, Mr. West, I'm Tom Lane with JD Computers."
(Smiles and pauses.)

Henry (2): (must get up and go to Tom in order to avoid being rude.)
"Hello, Mr. Lane. Have a seat please."
(said in a monotone.)

Tom (3): (takes seat to side of desk, immediately sits in his green signal posture.)
"Mr. West, I know that your time is very valuable. If I can have seven minutes of your attention, I'll be glad to show you why our Model 211 computer is better than any competitive model—better in price, in quality, and in service availability."
(Pauses.)

Henry (4): (tilts head slightly, leans forward, crosses his arms.)
"Well, alright. Go ahead, Mr. Lane."

Tom (5): "Thank you." (continues sitting in green position, uses open-handed gestures as he speaks.)
"Mr. West, I know how important it is to be sure you're buying a reliable product. Do you know Mr. Merdock of KB Appliances?"

Henry (6): (looks directly at Tom.)
"Yes, I know Bill Merdock."

Tom (7): (smiles and returns Henry's eye contact.)
"Mr. Merdock has had our Model 211 for 6 months now, and is very pleased with our product and our service. He said that

he would wholeheartedly recommend JD Computers to businesses like his, and yours Mr. West. You see, because we are a local (voice emphasis) company, we've been able to fill the needs for fast and reliable service much more efficiently than any other company (smile). Have you heard about our company before, Mr. West?" (nods head.)

Henry (8): (loosens up a little.)

"No. But I must say that I'm very leery of buying an 'off brand' computer."

Tom (9): (continues green signals, tilts head as Henry speaks.)

"I can understand your concern there, sir (open palm gesture). That's the reason why I believe this chart by *Computer World* Magazine will be of interest to you (pause). It shows what a good value our Model 211 provides in relation to other higher-priced, well-known models that have identical features to ours."

Henry (10): (shows more interest, sits up, smiles, wants to look at chart Tom holds.)

"I wasn't aware of any comparisons that included your #211, Mr. Lane. Let me see here . . ."

Tom (11): (points out specifics of price, features, number of service calls per month, etc. while holding onto the chart, then continues into his needs analysis while he has Henry's attention.)

Tom's patient handling of Henry's yellow signals, his own persistent use of green signals, and his opening statements and questions designed to perk up Henry's interest have succeeded in getting him into the next phase of his sales call. Below are the specific positive techniques Tom used to turn Henry's signals from yellow to green.

(1) Tom stops before he reaches Henry's desk, so that Henry is drawn away from his barrier (the desk). His pause puts the responsibility of the next move on Henry and indicates confidence (remember the discussion on fillers vs. silence, Chapter 4).

(2) Henry is sending out yellow signals—his greeting is brief and delivered in a monotone, and his unwillingness to come out from behind his desk is obvious.

(3) Tom takes a seat that will allow him to use his chart effectively when the time comes, and gives him a better view of Henry. He acknowledges that Henry's time is valuable and offers several customer benefits.

(4) Henry is becoming interested (tilts his head and leans forward), but is still signaling yellow (crossed arms, short reply to Tom's question).

(5) Tom doesn't mirror Henry's yellow signals and asks a question to lead Henry into a friendlier discussion by using the name of someone Henry knows.

(6) Henry shows more eye contact now and shows that he is an acquaintance of Mr. Merdock by using the familiar "Bill." Tom picks up on this and continues to use Mr. Merdock as a recommendation.

(7) Tom states that other businessmen "like" Henry have used and like his product, and talks about the benefits of his smaller company in comparison to the giants, putting Henry more at ease.

(8) Henry begins to show less reluctance to the call as he becomes convinced that Tom's product is worth considering. Although his yellow signals are less severe (he is less tight and tense), his verbal reply still indicates that he has reservations that must be dealt with.

(9) Tom acknowledges Henry's concern over a brand other than a well-known sure thing. He then produces reliable proof of his product's advantages. The chart, at this point, will serve to draw Henry closer to Tom, increasing his feeling of cooperation.

(10) Henry is now sending green signals. He is interested in the chart's information and is willing to listen to a further explanation of Tom's Model 211.

(11) Tom picks up on Henry's green signals and uses the momentum to go right into the next phase of his sales call.

The following sequence of photos represents what Tom saw as he scanned Henry for his nonverbal signals.

Henry's Nonverbal Signals

BODY ANGLE: straight, with
                hunched shoulders
FACE: frown, tight
ARMS: back
HANDS: clenched together
LEGS: crossed away from salesman

1.

Tom: "Mr. West, I know that your time
is valuable. If I can have
seven minutes of your attention. . . ."

BODY ANGLE: back slightly
FACE: uninterested
ARMS: back
HANDS: open
LEGS: crossed away from salesman

2.

Henry: Well, all right. Go ahead. . . ."

BODY ANGLE: forward
FACE: concerned
ARMS: forward moving
HANDS: open, pointed finger
LEGS: open

3.

Henry: ". . . I must say that I'm leery
of buying an 'off-brand' computer."

BODY ANGLE: straight
FACE: smiling, friendly
ARMS: away from body
            more relaxed
HANDS: one open, one
            gesturing
LEGS: open

4.

Henry: "I wasn't aware of any
comparisons that included
your #211. Let me see here. ..."

BASICS FOR OPENING A SALES CALL

The following are the major points to remember during the opening phase of your call. Your number one priority is to elicit green signals from your prospect so that you can continue on to a needs analysis.

- Unbuttoned jacket—conveys a friendly, open attitude.
- Sincere smile—shows confidence and enthusiasm.
- Solid stance—no swaying, distance of 1½ - 4 feet, 45° to 90° angle to the client, briefcase and arms at your side.
- Let the client come to you.
- Moderately firm handshake—vertical position, not overly energetic.
- Choose the best possible seating arrangement.
- Always use green signal sitting posture—sit forward in seat, lean forward slightly, legs and arms uncrossed, hands open, palms-up gestures, don't lean on the desk.
- Maintain eye contact.
- Listen to your client's statements and comments.
- Don't mirror yellow or red client signals.
- Continuously use the five-channel scan to gauge your progress.

Many salespeople take the opening phase of a sales call for granted. They assume that a handshake and a pleasant hello will do the job. And sometimes that's true. But it doesn't do the *best* job. A smooth, confident opening that relaxes your client and creates an interest in hearing more about your product or service gives you a much better chance of getting to your well-prepared presentation. Each step of the sales call builds momentum that will help you close the sale. Use all the energy you've got to get things rolling right away, and each step can be easier instead of harder to accomplish.

CHAPTER 7

Needs Analysis

In the next phase of your sales call, you want to discover your client's needs, motivations, and hidden concerns. Open gestures that show interest and attentiveness, as well as excellent listening skills, are absolute musts. If you gain the information you need, your presentation can be tailored to your client. Once you've established trust, your prospect will be receptive to hearing about your product or service.

OPEN VS. CLOSED QUESTIONS

Open questions give your clients a chance to explain their needs and concerns by asking for their opinions, expectations, preferences, judgements, or motivations. Closed questions offer little reason to expand on a one-word answer—it is either yes or no, this choice or that choice. Your objective during a needs analysis is to gain information to increase your chances for customizing your presentation to your prospect's specific needs.

Below, you will see the difference in results when you phrase the same question in a closed or open way.

Example One

Closed: "Is increased productivity important to you?"

Since the response is likely to be a simple yes or no, you have failed to find the reasons *why*. These may be vital for you to close the sale.

Open: "I was wondering about your expectations concerning productivity. How do you measure this in your operation?"

With this question, you will either find out that productivity is not a major concern, or why it is important.

Example Two

Closed: "Are you satisfied with your present insurance coverage?"

Again, you're likely to get a flat yes or no, or a qualified "I guess so."

Open: "If you could alter your current insurance coverage, without incurring any rate increases, how would you change it—what would you add or eliminate?"

Without the constraint of price, the client is likely to describe his "ideal policy" which you can use to your advantage in your presentation, playing up those areas he or she is most interested in.

Asking open questions takes practice. They require more thinking and concentration. Your choice of words and use of emphasis will lead to a productive discussion of the specific information you need.

Because open questions take some planning, we suggest that you develop two separate lists of questions. The first list will contain the questions you are using now. Write down as many questions as you can by remembering what you've asked clients during your last five or six calls. This will serve two purposes:

1. It will tell you whether you are currently using open or closed questions.

2. It will pinpoint the type of information you normally need to obtain from your clients.

Your second list will contain your new open questions. Find at least 10 new ways of asking about the client's needs so that you can customize your presentation to your client's specific situation. Say each of your questions out loud to determine which words need to be emphasized.

DISCOVERING YOUR BUYER'S MOTIVATIONS

Clients usually have a primary buying motive for selecting a particular product. Whether it's quality, the repair rate, compatibility, or emergency service, they want to hear about the features and benefits directly related to their specific concerns. They may "tune out" everything else you say. If what they want to hear (the dominant buying motive) is buried in the middle of your presentation, they might miss it completely.

By using a series of strategically sequenced open questions you will gain this vital information and avoid missing the buyer's hot button.

Step One—Exploring general buying motives

"Of all the products you can choose from, what interested you in. . . .?"

"Of all the products you've heard about, what feature or service interests you the most?"
The answer to these initial open questions will usually be very general. Now go on to help the client or customer define his main concern.

Step Two—Narrowing the focus

"It's interesting that you mention quality." PAUSE. "What do *you* (emphasis with tone of voice) mean by quality?"
The *you* emphasis is very important. You want to find out exactly what the customer means before you explain the product in detail. For instance, to one prospect quality may mean:

"I don't want it to break down in the first two weeks I've got it."
Another client may answer in response to the *same* question:

"The instructions can't be too complicated. If nobody can understand how to run the thing, it'll just sit there."
A third prospect may say:

"If I need a part, I don't want to be told that it's back-ordered."

Step Three—Probe for experiences

"That's interesting. Could you tell me more about it?"
or

"I'm glad you mention that. What happened?"
If you encourage your prospects to share the past experiences that have shaped their expectations, you'll know exactly how to sell to your new client.

The better you understand what motivates your clients to buy a product or service, the more you can tell them what they want to hear. Are they concerned about the availability of parts? Make sure to mention how easy it is to get replacements, offer to supply them with a "loaner" if there'll be an unexpected delay, or offer them statistics on product life early in your presentation.

Addressing your prospect's concerns and specific expectations before you launch into a prepared, formal presentation will maximize your chances for a strong close. Clients who feel that you will be discussing what *they* want to know, not just what *you* want to tell them, will follow your presentation with an open mind and a listening ear.

MATCH YOUR PROSPECT'S LANGUAGE

You can get additional clues about the type of information your clients want to hear by listening to their choice of words. Most people lean toward one of the three major modes of communicating.

1. Visual-oriented language.
2. Auditory-oriented language.
3. Action-oriented language.

They actually tell you how to phrase your statements and questions to get their attention.

Example One—Visual

Prospects who prefer visual information will use phrases like "That's *clear*," "I *see* what you mean," "Can you *show* that to me?" or "Can you *look* into that?" Charts, brochures, and seeing the actual product will gain the interest of these clients. During your needs analysis, begin using similar phrases. Also, make a mental note of the areas of your presentation that you can stress to make the most of the client's visual preference.

Example Two—Auditory

Customers who prefer auditory information use sound words such as "That *rings* a bell." "That doesn't *sound* quite right," "I don't think we're in *harmony* on this issue," or "They'll sure get a *bang* out of that." Anything that makes noise will interest this client—the pleasant click of a new machine, the soft chirping of modern telephone equipment, the quiet hum of an electronic typewriter. Also, these clients will be more attuned to your tone of voice, so concentrate on moderating your volume and using a good range of pitch. Make sure to include "sound" words in your own vocabulary.

Example Three—Action

Clients who desire action information use physical phrases as "We'll have to *kick* that idea around," "I don't *grasp* what you're saying," "I'll have to *lean* on my boss to get that okay'd," or "We could use a *shot* in the arm." These are the people who love demonstrations where they can try out a product—they want to touch it, do it, and hold onto it. Emphasize action words in your own speech and zero in on anything in your presentation that moves.

YOUR BASIC LISTENING POSTURE

Just as it is easier to sit in a green signal position if it is automatic, you are more likely to use a good listening posture if you have one ready to put into action. Showing your clients that you are paying attention while they are answering your questions is very important. It encourages them to continue talking, thus giving you additional information. So keep in mind the following gestures that help to convey your interest and use the ones that you feel most comfortable with.

- Slightly tilted head.
- Nodding with major points or in rhythm with the client's speech pattern.
- Slight leaning back in chair with head raised slightly—make sure to keep legs, arms, and hands *open* and move forward again to distinguish this from a defensive gesture.
- Good eye contact; a slight squint shows that you are considering what is being said.
- Avoid self-touching gestures—although clients may use chin-rubbing, lip-pulling and cheek-tapping when they are evaluating *your* statements, these gestures can also express uncertainty.
- Smile when *appropriate*; otherwise keep your lips slightly parted, and avoid frowning.
- Take notes—unless you have an excellent memory for details, you should jot down the client's needs, motivations, and concerns.

COMMUNICATE YOUR UNDERSTANDING

To conclude the needs analysis of your call, rephrase what the customer has said to show that you really were listening. Ask if you have accurately summarized his or her main concerns.

For example:

1. "Thank you Mr. Jones for sharing this information with me. (I *see*, I *hear*, I *gather*) from your comments that your needs call for (review needs). Would you say that's accurate?"

2. "Mrs. McNare, it (*looks* to, *sounds* to, *strikes*) me that you not only need increased production, but also need to reduce maintenance time. I'm glad you told me about this; now we can both review how our new product can help you to solve both problems."

IMPROVING YOUR LISTENING SKILLS

If you have difficulty summarizing your client's needs, even when you take notes, you may need to improve your concentration power. Listen with your eyes as well as your ears to get more meaning out of what is being said.

Ask yourself these questions while listening:

1. Is the client's body language consistent with what he or she is saying?
2. Does the client switch to a yellow or red signal when a specific topic comes up?
3. Can you tell by increased movements which topics the client is most enthusiastic about?

The following simple exercise will help you to fine-tune your visual and auditory listening skills:

Step One

Listen to the first three stories of the evening news. Then turn off the set and write on a pad of paper: a) the main theme of each story, and b) the visuals (film clips, or sketch/photo) used to illustrate the story.

Step Two

Listen to three more stories, but this time use a pad of paper to take notes while you watch. Now compare which method of notetaking provides you with more useful information.

A SAMPLE NEEDS ANALYSIS

In the following needs analysis scene of a sales call, list all the saleswoman's "wrong moves" and the signals her client is exhibiting on a separate sheet of paper.

Mary Jones sells office machines. She has opened her sales call, and has gotten a green signal from her client, Joan Ray, to continue. She is anxious to get right to her presentation while the prospect seems to be in a receptive mood.

THE SCENE

Mary (1): (uncertain about where to begin, clears her throat, crosses her ankles and tucks them under her chair.)

"Mrs. Ray, can you tell me, is cutting down on lost time for product repairs important to you?"

Joan (2): (leans forward and smiles.)

"Yes, it certainly is."

Mary (3): (hesitates, waiting for Mrs. Ray to say more, then continues with slightly slumped shoulders.)

"Are you having problems with the copy machines you're now using?"

Joan (4): (slightly impatient, grabs back of neck, crosses one arm, wonders where this is leading.)

"I'm not completely happy with what we've purchased in the past."

Mary (5): (looks down at desk, puts hands together, arms are tightly pulled against body.)

"Can you explain to me the types of problems you're having?"

Joan (6): (gestures with one arm while keeping the other close to her body.)

"If you could only see the copies some of our machines make—they're never clear."

Mary (7): (sits up, smiles.)

"Our line of office machines would give you a needed shot in the arm. They're the best machines on the market, they are very easy to use and most of our clients require very few service calls for repairs."

Joan (8): (closes up body posture.)

"I just can't see getting money for a new machine right now. When my budget is clearer, I'll give you a call."

Mary (9): (rejection shows all over her face, her whole body slumps.)

"I'm sure that if you had a chance to try out our new copier you'd find it's of excellent quality."

Joan (10): (stop gesture.)

"No, I'll think about it when our budgeting situation is a little brighter."

Mary got her client's interest when she started to discuss specific problems Joan is having with her present equipment. Unfortunately, Mary did not pick up Joan's choice of language, nor did she further explore Joan's need for clean copies.

Here is the anatomy of a missed sale:

(1) Mary sends out yellow signals by clearing her throat, crossing her ankles, and tucking them under her chair. She starts her needs analysis with a closed question.

(2) Joan is showing green signals and seems willing to give Mary information about her situation. If Mary had asked an open question, she might have had much more to say.

(3) Mary does not realize that she'd asked a closed question, and expects Joan to say more. When she doesn't, Mary becomes uncertain about what to do, and continues to give out yellow signals. Again, she asks a closed question.

(4) Now Joan is exhibiting yellow signals. She is probably reacting to Mary's yellow signals in addition to feeling impatient.

(5) Mary becomes defensive in response to Joan's yellow signals. She finally asks an open question. Joan must really need new machines to keep this sales call going.

(6) Joan opens up a little by gesturing with one arm. She is definitely a visual type. She uses the words *see*, *clear*, and *sight*. Her main concern seems to be poor-looking copies. Now would be an excellent time for Mary to *show* Joan samples of the crisp copies her machines can produce.

(7) Instead of showing concern for her customer's problems, non-verbally, Mary looks pleased that Joan is having difficulties. She sees a good

chance for a sale and launches into her regular sales pitch. She uses action and auditory vocabulary and fails to demonstrate that she's heard what Joan needs.

(8) Joan is bordering on a red signal. She continues to use visual phrases to describe her problem. Budgeting seems to be an excuse to get rid of Mary at this point.

(9) Mary's confidence decreases rapidly. Although she tries a last-ditch effort to perk up Joan's interest, she is sending out "Don't buy from me" signals. She is also still using action phrasing—if she had suggested that she could *show* Joan samples of work her machines produce instead of the action form of "trying out," she might have turned things around.

(10) Joan can't take any more and goes into a red signal. She continues to use visual words—*look, brighter*—as she ends the meeting.

This is the way Joan looked during the sales call. Mary could have gotten through her presentation and probably gone on to a close if she'd paid more attention to Joan's body language, improved her needs analysis skills, and showed appropriate open, concerned gestures to indicate her interest in helping Joan, not herself.

Joan's Nonverbal Signals

BODY ANGLE: forward
FACE: smiling, friendly
ARMS: open
HANDS: holding glasses

1.

Mary: ". . . is cutting down on lost time
for product repairs important to you?"

BODY ANGLE: straight, turned
                    away from seller
FACE: concerned, tense
ARMS: close to body
HANDS: grasping neck and arm

2.

Joan: "I'm not completely happy with
what we've purchased in the past."

BODY ANGLE: slightly forward
FACE: annoyed, animating words
ARMS: open
HANDS: pressing on desk and
                gesturing

3.

Joan: "If you could only *see* the
copies some of our machines
make—they're never clear."

BODY ANGLE: slightly back
FACE: serious, tense
ARMS: open
HANDS: stop gesture and
           holding chair arm

4.

Joan: "No, I'll think about it when
      our budgeting situation is
      a little brighter."

JOAN REVISITED

In the following sale, Mary exhibits more confidence and understands how to use the needs analysis to lead into a winning presentation that is tailored to her customer's individual requirements.

Please identify what Mary is doing correctly, and imagine the client signals she is responding to.

THE SCENE

Mary (1): (sits forward in chair, arms and legs uncrossed, smiles.)

"Mrs. Ray, I understand that you are not completely satisfied with your present office equipment. May I ask you how you see your specific needs at this time?"

Joan (2): (anticipates a series of unproductive questions, arms are crossed, looks serious.)

"All right."

Mary (3): (neutral expression, tilts head.)

"If you could have any machine you wanted, regardless of price, which feature would you be most interested in?"

Joan (4): (hand goes to chin, thinks for a minute.)
"Quality."

Mary (5): (nods, leans forward.)
"I see. Can you tell me what *you* mean by quality?"

Joan (6): (moves arm away from body, frown disappears.)
"I see it as a machine that produces crisp, clean copies without smudges or fuzziness."

Mary (7): (continues to nod and look interested.)
"What would be second on your list of important features?"

Joan (8): (looks more interested, is visibly less tense.)
"Low repair cost."

Mary (9): (uses open-hand gestures, nods.)
"It looks to me like you have had an interesting experience with an outrageous repair bill."

Joan (10): (smiles, uses open-handed gestures and leans forward.)
"As a matter of fact, I've seen several out-of-sight bills cross my desk recently."

Mary (11) (uses open-handed gestures and smiles.)
"Mrs. Ray, I appreciate your sharing this information with me. I can see that you envision a good quality copier that will require fewer repairs and one that will produce clean, sharp-looking copies. I would like to show you two things that will be of interest to you. First, a copy of our brochure that explains why our quality is superior and second, a few samples of what we can do for you to meet your needs."

Joan (12): (smiles, uses open-handed gestures and leans forward.)
"Why yes, I'd like to see what your product can do."

Mary can now slip right into her presentation. She has picked up Joan's visual vocabulary and has assured her that her needs for high quality and low repair costs are understood.

Here's what happened:

(1) Mary begins with a confident, green signal posture. She states the known reason for Joan's interest in new equipment and asks permission to inquire about Joan's specific needs.

(2) Joan remembers her last meeting with Mary, expects to have a difficult time, and signals yellow. Even her verbal agreement to listen to Mary's questions is testy.

(3) Mary looks interested and concerned as she asks an open question designed to discover Joan's priorities in seeking a new product.

(4) Joan has to think about her response, which gets her more involved in the sales call. She states the general feature of quality as her primary need.

(5) Mary moves forward and goes on to step two of her motivational questions to get specific information from Joan about her definition of "quality." She also uses the visual phrase "I *see*."

(6) Joan is becoming interested, although still somewhat reserved. She explains her needs in terms of crisp, clean copies without defects.

(7) Mary nods and continues showing interest in Joan's comments. She asks another open question about Joan's priorities.

(8) Joan has switched to a more open posture. She quickly replies to Mary's question.

(9) Mary uses green, open-handed gestures. She expresses sympathy for Joan's problems with repair costs by making a statement that gives Joan an opening for describing past bad experiences.

(10) Joan gives green signals and admits that she's had some high bills to pay lately.

(11) Mary continues giving green signals as she summarizes Mrs. Ray's priorities, then suggests providing visual proof of her copier's superiority.

(12) Joan begins to follow Mary's presentation with increased interest.

The following sequence of photos represents how Joan reacted to Mary this time (pages 136-137).

Joan's Nonverbal Signals

1. Joan: "All right."

BODY ANGLE: hunched forward
FACE: serious, suspicious
ARMS: tightly crossed
HANDS: holding onto arms

BODY ANGLE: hunched forward
FACE: serious, considering
ARMS: one crossed, one up
HANDS: to chin

2. Joan: "Quality."

BODY ANGLE: slightly forward
FACE: less tense, neutral
     expression
ARMS: open
HANDS: to chin

3.

Joan: "I see it as a machine that
produces crisp, clean copies
without smudges. . . ."

BODY ANGLE: slightly forward
FACE: friendly
ARMS: open
HANDS: open

4.

Joan: "Why yes, I'd like to see what
your product can do."

BASICS FOR DISCOVERING YOUR CLIENT'S NEEDS

A well-performed needs analysis will give you a tremendous advantage during your next step, the presentation. It provides you with information about the specific needs, dominant buying motivations, and individual concerns of your client. It tells you what type of information your client prefers—visual, auditory, or action. And it gives you a chance to gain your client's trust by showing that you care about what he or she has to say.

- Use open questions to gain information.
- Listen with your ears and your eyes.
- Continue to scan your client's nonverbal communication channels to plan your next move.
- Show concern and interest.
  a. Verbally—i.e. "I understand that _____ is very important to you."
  b. Vocally—use pauses, don't rush the pace, use the same type of language (visual, auditory, action) that the client uses.
  c. Nonverbally—tilt your head slightly, nod, use back and forth body motions, take notes.
- Thank the client for giving you the information you requested.
- Restate your client's specific needs, motivations, and concerns and use them to lead into your presentation.

To some salespeople, a needs analysis is an annoying, unnecessary delay in getting to their presentation. But the winning salesperson knows that you can't give a good presentation until you know *what* your clients are interested in, the *form* they prefer for receiving this information, and *why* it is important to them.

CHAPTER **8**

Presentation

The objective of your presentation is to persuade your prospects that you can fulfill their individual needs better than anyone else. By tailoring your verbal and nonverbal expressions to the individual client, and by using the information from your needs analysis, you will dramatically increase the impact of your presentation. Through the use of pauses and vocal emphasis combined with open gestures and eye contact you can effectively highlight your features and benefits. Use several trial closes during this phase of the call to set the stage for the final close.

CUSTOMIZE YOUR PRESENTATION

Your observations during the needs analysis will tell you, for example, that one client wants action information about operating costs and another prefers visual information about availability of service. A third client may want to hear auditory information about average product life. Even though the best part of your standard presentation is about another topic or a particular feature, you must target your words to what clients want to hear. Otherwise, you risk losing their interest. To get the greatest impact from your words remember to:

- Match your vocabulary to your client's visual, auditory, or action choice of words.

- Match your visual aids to your client's seeing, hearing, or doing preference.
- Stress the topics and features your client wants to hear about first and give them the most emphasis.

STATE BENEFITS

Features describe product characteristics. Benefits describe the customer's reasons for buying. Customers need to hear the main reasons for spending their company dollars. They want to know the effects on the bottom line—"What will it do for me to make it worth the cost? Why is this of value to me?"

Always match your customer benefits to your buyer's motivations. For example, the client who wants a "quality" product or service with national name recognition will love to hear that your company was listed with the top 10 corporations in a *Wall Street Journal* article. This information may seem obvious or unimportant to you but it will receive 100 percent of your client's attention. After you receive green signals in response to this benefit statement, you can remind the client that national name recognition means high resale value, proven service records, lower cost per operating hour, etc.

By targeting your product benefits to your customer's dominant buying motivations, you build a bridge between the customer's needs and the satisfaction he or she will experience by owning your product.

USE PERSUASIVE EYE CONTACT

Make sure that your clients are following you by visually leading them to the key benefits of your product. Your own eye movements clue in your clients to what is important.

VERBAL PRESENTATION POWER	NONVERBAL SELLING POWER
"Mr. Brown"	eye contact with client
"This office chair is coated with a stain and water resistant sealant."	eyes move to chair or picture in brochure

"I mention this . . ."	eyes move back to client
". . . because . . ."	direct eye contact
". . . it will not absorb correction fluids or beverages, and it is more durable than vinyl."	smile and observe prospect's reactions

While discussing product features, direct your customer's attention to your sales literature, spec sheet, or samples. Then look your customer straight in the eye as you state the benefits. Clients interpret eye contact as honesty. If you don't look at your clients while explaining benefits, they may get the impression that you don't believe in what you're saying. Scanning your clients for their reactions will tell you when to use trial closes.

USE POSITIVE PAUSES

During your presentations, most of your listening will be with your eyes, not your ears. Your pauses will give you time to "listen" to your prospects' body language. Look for their reactions to benefit statements and respond to yellow signals early to get back on the right track. Note their "interrupt gestures" before they verbalize their concerns and immediately ask open questions about what you've just discussed.

Use pauses to give the client more time to absorb your presentation. Although prospects can listen faster than you can speak, they may be thinking about something you've just stated and will miss your next statement. The pause tells them to switch gears and get ready for a new idea or topic. If they give a yellow signal, you'll know that they're not ready for you to continue.

Remember, pauses increase your credibility. Strategically placed pauses show self-confidence and assurance. People who are sure of what they're saying don't need to fill up silences with words and sounds.

MAINTAIN CONTROL OVER YOUR MATERIALS

Once your product or visuals leave your hands, you give up control of your presentation. Your client is free to be distracted from everything else you say. Use visual aids to your advantage:

- Hold onto brochures and spec sheets while pointing out key features and benefits. This allows you to direct the customer's attention to the important points of your presentation.

- Hold slides, transparencies and large visuals up high—your rationale can be explained as better lighting. The real objective is to get your prospect to stand and look up, which gets him or her away from the desk and into a more cooperative position. Your leadership will be enhanced by having the prospect follow your suggestions.

- Place your visuals out of sight when you are finished with them so that they don't draw the client's attention away from your following remarks.

- Use only clear and simple visuals. If they are too complicated, the customer may think that it's too much trouble to understand them. If you rely too heavily on visuals, you may give the impression that you really don't know your product and you're using diagrams and graphs as a crutch.

ASK OPEN QUESTIONS

Use open questions during your presentation to gather immediate feedback about how your presentation is going. Presentations do not follow the same structur as speeches. Open questions during this phase of the sale will provide you with the necessary information for deciding how your client wants to be sold. For example, after you've stated your customer benefits you could ask:

> "You mentioned earlier that cutting your operating cost is important to you. What is your objective opinion on this cost report?"

> "Can you tell me how this high resale value compares to the product you're using now?"

> "I was wondering how you rate this particular feature?"

> "Can you share your ideas on how this product/service could help you meet your needs?"

> "Could you refresh my memory for a moment? What did you say during our last conversation about needing a product that gives you fewer headaches. . . ?"

Questions involve the customer. An involved customer is more likely to sign an order.

KEEP THE CLIENT'S ATTENTION

Some customers have shorter attention spans than others, so you need to prepare some "grabbers" that will appeal to a number of personality types. During your needs analysis you can usually determine whether your customer is shy or outgoing, interested in prestige or concrete results, analytical or impulsive, a story lover or a fact fanatic. If you've listened carefully to what the client said, how he said it, and what he did nonverbally while he said it, you can choose from the following attention-getters:

1. **Analogies**—create vivid mental pictures by comparing your product/service or customer problem to a common experience.

Example: "Think of your present faulty equipment as a single weed (put up one finger) in a garden. The longer it's there, the more ground it takes over (spread hands apart), and the more money and time it takes to remove it (open palms to client)."

2. **Drama and Action**—feed the prospect's ego by telling the person how impressed everyone will be when your product/service is a success.

Example: "I can see you in a few months (tilt head and nod). Your secretarial pool is putting out *twice* (emphasis with voice and move hands to indicate a large stack of papers) as much work and *enjoying* (smile) it. Everyone's saying what a terrific decision you made on this equipment."

3. **Confront the Opposition**—acknowledge a problem and turn it into a benefit.

Example: "I agree that our price appears higher than the average (direct eye contact), but when you figure in the longer product life (open-hands gesture) and reduced maintenance costs (bring hands closer together), you're actually saving money (raise hands, palms toward client)."

4. **Immediacy**—convince the client that now is the time to buy.

Example: "I'll have to increase the cost of this item (shake head slightly, look of concern) when the new price list comes in, and it was due yesterday (direct eye contact, hand to chest)."

5. **Prestige**—offer the prospect a better reputation for himself and his company.

Example: "This product will increase (open arms, palms out toward client) your productivity by 15 percent (emphasize 15 percent with hand gestures and voice) within just 4 (use fingers) months, pulling you well in front of the competition."

6. **Convenience**—assure the customer of readily available assistance.

Example: "Our service technicians are on call 24 hours a day (emphasize 24 hours a day with nod of head and voice)."

7. **Similarity**—show your understanding of the client's needs by mentioning your own or another customer's experience with the product.

Example: "I've got one of these at home (point to sample, brochure), and even my kids (raise eyebrows, emphasize with voice) have figured out how it works."

8. **Caring**—demonstrate that you're concerned about your client's reputation.

Example: "One of our customers had a key component fail during a peak production period (direct eye contact). Our service department had it fixed within 3 (use fingers) hours of her call to us, and the warranty covered all the costs (sweeping hand motion)."

These attention-getters don't just perk up your customer's interest. They give you the opportunity to 1) vary the tone of your voice because they are not cut and dried facts, 2) use a broader range of gestures for emphasis, and 3) put you on a friendlier, more relaxed level with your client than a "formal" presentation allows.

SMALL GROUP AND LARGE AUDIENCE PRESENTATIONS

Up to this point, we have focused on sales calls to a single client. Yet, there will probably be times when you will give a presentation to a group of clients. Although you will not be able to tailor your presentation to every individual, you can:

- Adjust your tone of voice and gestures to the audience size—as the group increases in size, increase your volume, and widen and intensify your gestures.
- Use pauses effectively to give your audience an impression of a self-confident, well-organized, honest professional.
- Create a bridge between features and benefits according to the particular group's needs and concerns.
- Scan the group as a whole—do you have most of the group's interest? Eye contact with at least half of the group at any one

time is critical. Is the majority of the group communicating green signals?

- Include a variety of attention-getters to grab the interest of those who are becoming bored and showing yellow signals.
- Ask pertinent, open questions at key points in your presentation instead of leaving the question-and-answer session until last.

KEEP CLOSING

Whenever a client exhibits a green signal or intensifies a green signal in response to a stated customer benefit, try for a close. Until your client hears about how his key needs will be satisfied, the close will not be successful. Use "trial closes" as you receive green signals in response to your explanation of key features and customer benefits to prepare for your final close.

A SAMPLE PRESENTATION

While reading and imagining the following presentation, think about how the salesman could improve his approach.

Mark Reed is thrilled with his new product presentation. He is sure it's a pitch that just can't lose. He opens in a friendly manner, receives what he interprets as a green signal, and begins his presentation.

THE SCENE

Mark (1): (grabs briefcase from floor, legs are crossed away from client.)

"I've got some fascinating statistics here that will really impress you with our new product line."

Jane (2): (lowers glasses skeptically, keeps one arm crossed.)

"Is that right?"

Mark (3): (he rises to put briefcase on desk.)

"I'll just get . . ."

Jane (4): (phone rings, she answers it, sees Mark about to put his briefcase on her desk and points to the other chair.)

"Please put that over there Mr. Reed. Excuse me, Mr. Jones, what did you say about . . ."

(Jane talks for a few minutes then hangs up.)

Mark (5): (takes out visuals, hands brochure to Jane.)

"Now here is something I'm sure you'll be interested in. As you can see here (points and leans across desk) our increases in productivity levels have been tremendous over the last few . . ."

Jane (6): (raises hand slightly to interrupt, when Mark keeps going she verbally interrupts.)

"But Mr. Reed, I'm concerned about limiting operating costs right now."

Mark (7): (abruptly sits back down, leaving brochure in Jane's hands.)

"Of course, Mrs. Pope. Now as you see on the back page of our brochure, our automatic shutoff valves save you from wasted utility costs and reduce the number of employees needed to monitor the equipment."

(Mark is not hiding his tension over not finishing his planned presentation very well nonverbally or vocally, although he does switch to the topics Jane wants to hear about. He sounds a bit short, swings his leg, and scratches his shoulder.)

Jane (8): (she is wary of what Mark says because his body does not show her that he is being honest and sincere—something isn't quite right. Her yellow signals are about to change to red if Mark doesn't relax soon.)

"I doubt that this feature would save us much over our present system. Our previous supplier promised us lower costs too, but after we bought it, our costs *increased*. They're now three times higher than before."

Mark (9): (becomes flustered and grabs his briefcase to look for another document.)

"Mrs. Pope, that's impossible. I can show you . . . let me prove this point . . ."

Jane: (10): (angrily points her finger.)

"Mr. Reed, don't tell me what's impossible. I just don't have time for this nonsense today. I'll keep this brochure and give you a call. Thank you."

Mrs. Pope's red signals and verbal comments have prevented Mark from continuing and he is soon out the door. Mark ignored Jane's signals and made quite a few errors nonverbally, although he tried to address Jane's concerns in words.

(1) Mark is sending out yellow signals—legs crossed away from his client, movements too quick—while not picking up on his client's yellow signals (Jane probably smiled politely but signaled yellow with other nonverbal channels). Mark's reference to statistics is not specific enough to catch Jane's interest.

(2) Jane is justifiably skeptical of this salesman as he launches into an obviously prepared pitch. Her yellow signals include looking over her glasses, one arm tightly crossed, and an erect, tense body. Even her brief response to Mark's statement expresses her doubts about the usefulness of any information he has to offer.

(3) Mark should have opened his briefcase on his lap or on the other chair. Now he has invaded Jane's territory and will intensify her yellow signals. He does not ask any open questions to grab Jane's interest before trying to present her with his statistics.

(4) If Jane really wanted to hear Mark's presentation without interruption, she could have asked to have her calls held. Instead, she takes the call, reprimands Mark with a pointing finger and an annoyed expression, and then apologizes to the caller for the interruption.

(5) Mark makes several mistakes at this point: he hands over the brochure, remains standing (implies aggression, domination), and again invades Jane's space by leaning too far over the desk to point out the information he thinks is important. He is also stressing productivity, while Jane is interested in other aspects of the product's potential.

(6) Jane becomes increasingly frustrated with Mark's lack of concern for her individual needs and his lack of attention to her subtle signals.

(7) Mark switches over to a discussion of a feature to reduce operating costs, which probably could be very effective if not coupled with so many negative signals (legs crossed, leg swinging, self-touching.)

(8) Jane's signals are now changing to red. She is skeptical of Mark's remarks because his body language doesn't seem to fit his words.

(9) Mark lets his own frustration over the situation show through his "I give up" hand gestures and his grab at the briefcase.

(10) At this point the sales call has become a battle of wills and Jane has the power to banish Mark from her office. Jane points her finger, looks angry, thrusts her body forward, clenches her fist, and ends the call.

Here is a visual representation of this sales call. Mark's complete lack of consideration pushed Jane to her limit. No matter what Mark says to verbally describe the features Jane is interested in, he cannot overcome such defensive, frustrated body language. (See pages 148-149.)

Jane's Nonverbal
Signals

BODY ANGLE: upright
FACE: granny glance
ARMS: close to body
HANDS: grasping arm and
              glasses

1.   Mark: "I've got some fascinating statistics
                   here that will really impress you. . . ."

BODY ANGLE: upright
FACE: annoyed, tense
ARMS: gesturing
HANDS: pointing and holding
              phone

2.   Jane: "Please put that over there. . . ."

BODY ANGLE: upright
FACE: skeptical, tense
ARMS: close to body
HANDS: holding brochure

Mark: "Now here is something I'm   3.
sure you'll be interested in. . . ."

BODY ANGLE: thrust forward
FACE: angry
ARMS: gesturing
HANDS: pointing, fist

Jane: ". . . don't tell me what's impossible."   4.

JANE REVISITED

After a careful needs analysis, Mark listens attentively as Jane discusses why she is interested in his product, and restates her needs and concerns. As he gains Jane's interest and trust, he watches for a green signal. At this point he begins his presentation:

THE SCENE

Mark (1): (legs uncrossed, leans forward slightly.)

"I'm glad you mentioned that you're interested in reducing operating costs. I'd like to show you specifically which features of our new product can meet your needs in this area. Have you heard about our Model 4-BX?"

Jane (2): (leans forward, looks friendly and interested.)

"Actually, one of my people talked to me about it just the other day."

Mark (3): (places briefcase on chair beside himself, takes out materials he will need, speaks while he is getting things ready.)

"I thought you might have seen some comments on it because EMR Corporation has just purchased one and I understand you do quite a bit of business with them. They're evidently very pleased with our product."

Jane (4): (still exhibiting open, interested gestures.)

"Can you provide me with the names of other companies who've tried this product? It's so new that I'd like to see how it's doing before we consider such a costly expenditure."

Mark (5): (leans forward with brochures in hand.)

"We've anticipated your reaction and have printed up some recommendations from other companies for you to look at. As you can see, the automatic control system has been a great benefit to our customers. It not only saves time (pause), it also cuts down on operating costs."

(as Jane leans forward to look at the visuals, Mark scans her for any early yellow signals. He notices that she has drawn one arm close to her body and takes precautionary measures.)

"Let me ask you this—are there any special considerations that you can see that might limit your use of this product?"

Jane (6): (taps finger, sits up some.)

"Well, I was wondering how compatible this would be with our present system. We simply can't afford to replace everything at once."

Mark (7): (shows interest and concern for Jane's reservations, nods head.)

"I see that you've planned a gradual updating of your equipment. I know that our service people will be more than happy to adapt our product to your present specifications, so that you won't have to replace any more equipment than you need to. You'll be pleased to know that we guarantee that compatible parts will be available for the life of the product."

Jane (8): (gets out a booklet listing tables of specifications.)

"That's really interesting, Mr. Reed. Let me show you just what we need."

(Mark gets out a pad and pen, and writes down some information. Jane uses open-handed gestures to indicate her willingness to continue to discuss the product in more detail.)

From this point on, Mark discusses only those aspects of his product that Jane is interested in, even though his usual discussion of other features has not been covered. He continues to deal with Jane's occasional yellow signals, changing them back to green, and uses several trial closes before moving on to the final close.

Here are the specific positive moves Mark made:

(1) Mark begins his presentation when he has gotten the "go ahead" from Jane's green signals. He uses a green signal posture himself and immediately relates his presentation to Jane's specific interests. He also asks an open question to involve Jane in the discussion while he prepares his materials.

(2) Mark uses a visual term to phrase his next comment. He also uses an attention-getter, referring to another satisfied customer that Jane knows.

(4) Jane is still interested, and asks a question about referrals. Even though her body language is open (from what Mark can see) she is being cautious about this new product, and moves her arm closer to her.

(5) Mark immediately offers to provide the information Jane desires, shows his concern about her needs by having anticipated the request, and pauses between giving his two benefit statements. He also scans Jane for any further reservations. He picks up a yellow signal and asks an open question to bring Jane back into a discussion and discover her concerns.

(6) Jane is thinking about what she needs as she taps her finger. She expresses her concern about compatibility.

(7) Mark shows by his body language and his words that he understands Jane's concern. He reassures her of the product's compatibility and long-range usefulness.

(8) Jane begins to feel better about the product and is ready to start a more detailed discussion of product specifications. Jane's open-handed gestures signal her willingness to continue the sales call.

Here is a sequence of photos that shows what happened visually:

**Jane's Nonverbal
Signals**

BODY ANGLE: forward
FACE: friendly
ARMS: open
HANDS: holding glasses

1.   Mark: ". . . they're evidently very pleased
                with our product."

BODY ANGLE: forward
FACE: interested
ARMS: open
HANDS: holding glasses

Mark: "We've anticipated your reaction and
have printed some recommendations
from other companies."

2.

BODY ANGLE: forward
FACE: interested
ARMS: closer to body
HANDS: touching brochure

Mark: ". . . are there any special considerations
that you can see that might limit
your use of this product?"

3.

4.

BODY ANGLE: forward
FACE: friendly
ARMS: open
HANDS: open palm out,
                holding booklet

Jane: "That's really interesting. Let
me show you what we need."

BASICS FOR PERSUASIVE PRESENTATIONS

Your presentation needs to put you and your product in the best possible light. To do this, you must emphasize the features that give your clients the benefits they desire. Flexibility is the key. As your presentation progresses, monitor your clients through scanning and questioning to make sure you stay on track.

- Begin a presentation only when the client gives you a green signal.
- Continue to use green signals yourself.
- Translate product features into customer benefits by using their choice of vocabulary and emphasize what they want to hear, not what you have prepared.
- Continue to scan for early yellow signals.
- Ask open questions to uncover hidden reservations.
- Don't invade the client's space by placing your briefcase on the desk, or leaning too far across the desk.

- Use pauses when speaking, to emphasize points and convey confidence and conviction.
- Use eye contact to direct your client's attention to the main benefits of your product.
- Maintain control of your visual aids
- Use a number of trial closes—after your customer shows steady green signals in response to your benefit statements.

The best presentation in the world will lose the sale if it is not tailored to the individual client's needs. Once you have presented the information your clients want in the way they want to hear it, you'll get their green "go ahead" signal which earns you the right to close the sale.

CHAPTER 9

Objections

What does your body communicate when a prospect says: "Your price is too high?" Think of your last sales call and try to remember specifics—your body angle, facial expression, the position of your arms, hands, and legs. Most salespeople—80 percent of those videotaped during practice sessions—show negative changes in their body postures when hearing objections.

When a client sees yellow signals, such as crossed arms and legs, head-scratching, swaying from side to side, nose-rubbing, and fingers under the collar, your problems are intensified. The prospect may think: "Ah, now I've come to the weak spot!" Even though your verbal reply is flawless, your nonverbal expressions may communicate: "I'm uncomfortable about this," or "I don't know if I will be able to convince you about buying from me."

Salespeople who communicate negative nonverbal signals after hearing the prospect's objection fail to recognize that 99 percent of all customer objections are preceded by yellow signals (note: the only exception is the "teaser objection" which is explained later). Therefore, the best time to deal with an objection is before it is stated.

But the best way of handling objections is prevention. If you've applied the techniques outlined in the previous chapters, and if you've handled all yellow signals, your customized product presentation should naturally end with the close.

If you do hear an objection, relax. You don't need to answer right away. Try rephrasing the objection instead, so you'll find out what the customer really means. You can take the stress out of selling by applying verbal and nonverbal selling power to turn objections into orders.

Here are nine types of customer objections with specific suggestions on how to best handle them.

TEASER OBJECTIONS

These are most likely to come up when the sales call has gone very well. If you have dealt with yellow signals promptly and thoroughly, clients may be ready to close, but ask for a little push. A friendly summary of your product or service benefits, and an assurance that this really is the best deal for their money, may be all they need.

Even though teaser objections don't represent real problems, they should not be taken lightly. A defensive reaction, an overly confident attitude, or an attempt to belittle your client's teaser objection can jeopardize your chances of making the sale.

Some body language clues for teaser objections are:

BODY ANGLE:	body leaning toward you
FACE:	smiling, relaxed, good eye contact
ARMS:	open, gesturing or relaxed on desk
HANDS:	open, relaxed, palms-toward-you gestures
LEGS:	uncrossed

In other words, the five-channel scan will reveal green signals. You will also notice that a client's tone of voice will seem friendly and calm, rather than hostile and agitated.

Here are some visual examples of token objections:

Example

Buyer: "I can't see how you can get away with charging so much."
Seller: "I agree that our price is higher than the average, but only initially. Because of the longer product life and low maintenance costs we've discussed, this product is actually cheaper than similar models."

Example

Buyer: "Aren't we taking a big risk buying a product that isn't made by a well-known company?"
Seller: "We feel that we'll soon have increased name recognition—not because we spend a lot on advertising and then have to charge higher

"I can't see how you can get away with charging so much."

"Aren't we taking a big risk buying a product that isn't made by a well-known company?"

prices, but because our satisfied customers tell others about our quality and excellent prices. And our warranties cover more parts for a longer period of time than better-known products. So actually a purchase from us is *less* risky."

You may already have stated all these benefits to your client. But summing up benefits using different words will make them stand out in your buyer's mind. It is usually a good idea to keep a few benefits as reserves for this type of situation. Then you not only reinforce what the client has heard, but peak his interest once more.

In brief, you should react to teaser objections by:

- Using green signals.
- Acknowledging the client's objections.
- Restating and adding to your list of customer benefits.
- Continuing to scan your client for yellow signals which indicate a more serious objection.

STALLING

There are two types of stalls. Each requires a different approach, so it is important for you to accurately read your prospect's body language before dealing with this type of objection.

Type#1—The Passive Stall

Some people hate to make decisions. No matter how convinced they are of a product's worth, they will try to postpone committing themselves to a purchase. They need to be assured that making the decision will benefit them more than *not* making it.

You will have to be patient with a customer who uses this type of objection. Don't take his comments lightly, don't become frustrated and show yellow signals, and don't rush him.

Nonverbal messages to look for include:

BODY ANGLE:	rigid and upright, or leaning back or away from you slightly
FACE:	tense, puzzled, lip-biting, little eye contact

ARMS: crossed or held close to body
HANDS: fingers to lips or chin, involved in
                             pipe rituals or playing with objects
                             on desk
LEGS: crossed or pressed together, foot
                             swinging, tapping or actual pacing

These yellow signals indicate that the client is experiencing inner conflict over making a decision. In this situation, open questions will bring this conflict out into the open. Respond to the customer's comments in a direct, helpful manner and then pause. You want to give the client time to think through doubts and uncertainties so that he or she can verbalize them. Trying to rush passive clients can make them retreat. Pressure will result in the client deciding to make no decision at all (for you, this probably means a negative decision) rather than make a poor purchase out of haste.

Example

Buyer: "I want to think about it."
Seller: "Perhaps I can help you. What are the points you are still uncertain about?"

Example

Buyer: "I don't buy anything until I sleep on the decision first."
Seller: "I understand that you need time to consider your decision. I'd be interested in hearing your thoughts about the reasons for and the reasons against buying now."

Clients who are having difficulty making a decision should not be told that the price will go up "tomorrow" or "any day now." A time deadline will only add to their feeling of panic. Reassurance and understanding will work much more effectively.

You can communicate your interest in helping the client make a good decision in these ways:

- Use green signals—stress open-palms gestures and hand-to-chest gestures.
- Acknowledge the client's concerns about making a decision.
- Probe for the underlying reasons for the stall.
- Address your prospect's specific uncertainties and restate your customer benefits.
- Don't try to close while the customer is still sending out yellow signals.

Type #2—The Active Stall

When a prospect has been communicating green signals throughout the sales call but balks at making a final commitment when you attempt to close, you are faced with an "active stall." The client needs a new request for action before he or she will agree to signing the deal.

Nonverbal signals will show:

BODY ANGLE:	forward
FACE:	friendly
ARMS:	open
HANDS:	open-palms gestures
LEGS:	uncrossed, or casually crossed

Instead of responding to your client's statement directly, and reacting with yellow signals, persuade your prospect to order now by asking about his opinion of the pros and cons of buying your product, and then restate the benefits of making a decision *today*.

Example

Buyer: "I'm just not sure that we can afford this product right now."
Seller: "I realize that this is a fairly large investment. Yet, from what we've discussed earlier, I sincerely believe that our product can meet all of your expectations, *and* save you the trouble of having to buy (more machinery, additional services, upgraded equipment) for many years."

Example

Buyer: "I think it would be better to wait a few days, I might get a better deal."

Seller: "I understand how you feel; however, I can assure you that the cost of this item has been unchanged for the last six months. Right now most of our competitors have already instituted a price increase, so by buying today you'll benefit from our lowest rate. If you choose to wait, you'll run the risk of paying much more."

Example

Buyer: "It isn't the right season to buy your product. I don't know why you people come around during our slow period."

Seller: "That's exactly why I'd like to talk to you now. You're not in a rush, with an already overloaded schedule, and we can plan your needs so that sufficient products are available when it *is* time to buy."

After you have summarized the reasons for buying, you can use one of the appropriate closes listed in the next chapter. You can get an active staller to take action by:

- Refusing to back out of the call ("I'll come back tomorrow, etc.).
- Using your own green signals while restating the customer benefits.
- Pressing for a close.

PRICE OBJECTIONS

Price objections *appear* to be valid reasons for not buying. When the customer is a shrewd bargainer, you must meet his or her resistance with a well-rounded response.

Example

Buyer: "Your price is way out of line."
Seller: "How are you comparing the price?"
Buyer: "It simply costs much more than other similar brands."
Seller: "We are in a higher price bracket, yet our sales were over $4 million last year. We couldn't sell at that rate unless we offered our customers quality and benefits that make our products cheaper over the long-run."

Example

Buyer: "I can get almost the same product 10 percent cheaper from another company. If you cut your price, I'll give you the order."
Seller: "It wasn't my impression that your products are the cheapest in your own industry. Our policy is to offer our best price first and give new customers the same deal we give our repeat purchasers."

Here, the seller didn't disagree with the price objection. But he turned it aside by focusing on an alternate reason for buying—long-term value.

Price objections lead most salespeople to react defensively, so remember to:

- Continue signaling green to your prospect.
- Don't defend your price directly—turn the objection into a probe for more specific information.

- Don't disagree with the price objection—focus on an alternate reason for buying (product life, value, etc.)

LACK-OF-FUNDS OBJECTIONS

In this situation, the prospect is not objecting to the product's price, but states that there just isn't enough room in his budget for the purchase. To overcome this objection you must probe to discover the following information:

- How is the budget determined?
- Who is responsible for authorizing expenditures?
- Who has the authority to override the budget limits?
- Which departments have excess funds that can be used for extraordinary purchasing opportunities?

Example

Buyer: "I don't have the budget for that right now."
Seller: "Can you tell me how your funds are allocated for this type of product?"

Example

Buyer: "I can't go beyond this year's budget."
Seller: "I realize that this is a special situation. Who could authorize increased funding for such an excellent opportunity where the product can pay for itself within the next 15 months?"

Example

Buyer: "My budget was cut back this year so I'll have to wait."
Seller: "If I could show you a way that you could earn back what you'll be spending this year on the lease plan, would you be interested?"

Budgets are not set in stone. But sometimes the client you are dealing with does not have the authority to make changes or take advantage of a good deal on his own. Discover who *can* alter or add to the budget.

Use the following techniques for dealing with "lack-of-funds" objections:

- Continue to send out green signals.
- Ask probing questions to gain specific information about funding procedures and options.
- Restate the money benefits your clients will receive from buying your product.

MISUNDERSTANDINGS

These commonly occur when the client is:

- Unfamiliar with technical terms.
- Unaware of your company's superiority in a particular product line or service.
- Uncertain of such product benefits as optional coverages, extended warranties, ability to obtain replacement parts, etc.

Example

Prospect: "I don't believe that this drug will improve my patients' conditions."
Seller: "Can you explain what you mean by that?"
Prospect: "We're dealing with an incurable disease here!"
Seller: "I realize that we can only offer relief from discomfort, not a cure. With our product, your patients will experience fewer side-effects than from the drugs currently on the market with the same amount of pain relief."

Example

Prospect: "I don't think our people are ready to get into word processing just yet. The typewriters work fine, and they are less complicated."
Seller: "I understand how you feel. Many of my clients had similar reservations before investing in these timesaving units. However, they realized that word processors are really as easy to use as a TV set—a few simple steps will get you good results without your needing to know about the advanced technology that makes them run. And they'll save so much time, you'll wonder how you ever got along without them."

Reinforcing your statements with visuals, testimonials, and positive body language will help to clear up the misunderstanding. Arguing or drawing attention to the customer's ignorance may "win" the discussion, but won't win the sale.

PRODUCT PROBLEMS

Client objections and a closed attitude can stem from a lack of trust in your product. Discovering the specific reasons for these doubts will allow you to discuss particular benefits that will eliminate or compensate for the prospect's objection.

Example

Buyer: "I'm not sure that your product is reliable."
Seller: "Hm . . . what makes you say that?"

Instead of proving your customers wrong, ask them to explain what makes them think that they're right.

Example

Buyer: "I just can't afford to go with a model without a service contract."
Seller: "You're obviously looking for a quality product that will give you a bare minimum of problems. Since we've designed our product in a modular way, your operator can exchange any component within five minutes and replace it with a new unit from our parts warehouse. This way you save 18 percent from the purchase price."

When you are confronted with an objection that specifically relates to your product:

- Continue to use green signals—stress evaluation gestures such as head tilting, nodding, leaning back slightly to listen and then move forward.
- Ask open questions to get a more detailed description of the problem or offer information that will remove the prospect's doubts.
- Don't try to close until your client gives you a green signal.

COMPANY PROBLEMS

Sometimes it is the reputation or size of your company that worries the client and keeps him from closing the deal. An objection based on your company may be stated directly or hinted at with doubts about the availability of parts, service, or the company's short history.

Example

Buyer: "I need a supplier that I can keep using for many years."
Seller: "I'm glad you mentioned that, because we've recently signed on a number of top firms for standing orders and they've expressed complete confidence in us. (Pause.) Here is a list of referrals."

Example

Buyer: "I need to be sure that I can get replacement parts a few months down the road."
Seller: "Even though our company is small, we've been in this business for (_____ years), providing reliable parts and service. And because we discontinue fewer products than larger companies, you've actually got a better assurance of obtaining needed parts in the future."

If you receive an objection that is based on your company:

- Continue to use green signals—stress evaluative gestures to show your concern.
- Acknowledge the prospect's lack of trust.
- Demonstrate, via your open gestures and the use of referrals or other materials, that your company is trustworthy.

PROBLEMS WITH YOU

Prospects who've had bad experiences with salespeople in the past usually display extremely negative signals and refuse to open up to a seller. Before you decide that the problem is your own and not your client's past biases, try to turn aside the objection.

Example

Buyer: "I just don't have time to listen to any more."
Seller: "I can save you time. In only five minutes (I can *show* you/ you will *hear*/ I can *demonstrate*) how our product will save you time and money in your operation."

When this approach doesn't work, find out if there is a personal problem with your approach to the client.

Example

> *Buyer:* "Your product sounds okay, but I'm going to have to give this decision more consideration."
> *Seller:* "Is it something about me that prevents you from doing business with our company?"
> (If the answer is a hedge, or a yes, you can continue by saying): "I'd be glad to put you in touch with another representative if you prefer. Our product and our company are extremely reliable and I'd hate for you to lose the benefits of a purchase."

Personality conflicts occur in sales situations just as they do in other aspects of life. If your choice is to lose the sale for yourself, or lose it for your company, offer to provide the client with another company contact. Your understanding, openness, and undefensive attitude may win you the sale anyway.

UNEXPECTED CHANGES IN CLIENT COMPANY SITUATIONS

Suppose you have had a preliminary meeting with a client. You've done a thorough needs analysis and a tailored presentation, but needed to provide the client with more information before he would close the deal. When you call on the client with this information in hand, you discover that the company has been reorganized, or the budgets have been changed, or there is a new person in charge of handling contracts for your product. What should you do?

Start from scratch. Thank the client for telling you about the changes in the company and begin exploring the company's new needs. Although the company may not have the *same* needs as it did before, it may have additional or different needs now.

Example

> *Buyer:* "I'm afraid the deal we talked about last week just won't work now. I've been moved to another department and the new guy in charge of purchasing refuses to take on this contract on my say so."
> *Seller:* "Thank you for telling me about this change. I certainly understand your replacement's need to discuss this purchase himself. Can you give me his name and number so that I can arrange to call on him?"

Example

Buyer: "Our company just went through an unexpected merger. Right now, we just don't need a contract like the one we discussed."
Seller: "Certainly changes in your company's structure will change your needs. Can we talk about the company's new status so that I can help you meet your new requirements?"

SAMPLE REACTIONS TO OBJECTIONS

Doug Bley has just finished his presentation to Jack Lowe. Doug knows that he lost Jack's interest once or twice but he's sure that Jack really needs his product. Just when Doug thinks that all signals are green and he should close the sale, Jack brings out an objection.

THE SCENE

Doug (1): (feet tucked under chair, leans far forward.)

"Since you're understandably interested in price, Mr. Lowe, there's another benefit I'd like to mention. We have a special arrangement with First Colony Bank for obtaining excellent loan terms with a prepayment option."

Jack (2): (friendly look, leans forward, raises one hand slightly.)

"It seems to me that you could still come down on that quote you gave me."

Doug (3): (feet go farther under the chair, leans on the desk with his forearms, uses index finger for emphasis.)

"I can assure you that this is the best price we've offered this year. The benefits of the automatic regulation system and override switch for increased safety of your employees, plus the decreased repair costs for you, will actually cost you less than a brand with only half the features over the long-run."

Jack (4): (shows expression of concern and doubt, finger goes to mouth, hand presses down on desk.)

"Yes, yes, there are a lot of benefits but can't the base price be reduced? I don't know whether I can fit this into my budget."

Doug (5): (leans back, crosses legs.)

"Our bank can certainly arrange your financing so that some of your costs fall into the next fiscal year, Mr. Lowe."

Jack (6): (continues touching his lips and nods slightly.)

"I'm going to have to think about this some more, Mr. Bley."

Doug (7): (sits back farther, crosses his arms.)

"I've been authorized to use this price list through Thursday. It would be a shame for you to miss this excellent price. Most of our competitors have already instituted a 7 percent increase. A decision now will save you money."

Jack (8): (raises finger to Doug, turns away slightly.)

"No, I won't be rushed into this. I need more input on how the system works before I make a final decision."

Doug (9): (puts one arm over back of chair, hands are clasped.)

"I'd be glad to give you some more detailed information, Mr. Lowe. I can have it here today if you'd like."

Jack (10): (goes to a stop gesture with his hands, face is tense.)

"That won't be necessary. I'll be in touch later in the week if we decide to go with your firm."

Doug let a minor objection surprise him. Things went downhill until Jack had progressed to real problems that he might not have worried about if Doug had been more reassuring and less pushy.

Here are the problems Doug had:

(1) He is not as well-balanced as he would be if his feet were flat in front of him. Doug's statement, taking him into a close, does stress the concerns that Jack has mentioned.

(2) Jack is leaning toward a sale, but wants to be sure he's been offered the salesman's best price. If he'd received a satisfactory reply from Doug, he'd probably have closed the deal.

(3) Doug is unprepared for an objection from Jack, who is still exhibiting green signals. He reacts a bit overaggressively by leaning too far forward and invading Jack's space by placing his forearms on Jack's desk. He verbally reassures Jack about the price, but is sending out warning signals with his body language.

(4) Jack is beginning to show doubt about this purchase. He wonders whether Doug is being completely truthful with him.

(5) Doug now retreats, showing defensive body language. He replies directly to the stall, instead of making reassuring statements about benefits, giving Jack some time to think, or asking open questions.

(6) Jack continues to show doubt. He is wary of Doug's continued push to close quickly.

(7) Doug continues to increase the intensity of his negative body language (moves farther back, crosses arms). He pressures Jack with a deadline and continues to discuss price instead of benefits. The "time urgency" close shouldn't be used when the client has shown a need for time to think.

(8) Jack is now showing yellow, bordering on red signals. The pressure of Doug's prodding and pushing is increasing his doubts about making a decision today. Now other uncertainties are occurring to him.

(9) Doug offers more information and shows his willingness to get it right away, but his body language is still too negative to reassure Jack.

(10) Jack gives up and goes to a red signal. He is now determined not to make a decision today.

The following sequence of photos shows Doug's mishandling of Jack's objections:

Jack's Nonverbal Signals

BODY ANGLE: leaning forward
FACE: friendly
ARMS: open
HANDS: gesturing and hidden

1.   Doug: "We have a special arrangement
        with First Colony Bank for
        obtaining excellent loans. . . ."

BODY ANGLE: leaning forward
FACE: doubtful, skeptical
ARMS: open
HANDS: fingers to mouth and
       pressing down on desk

Doug: "I can assure you that this is   2.
the best price we've offered. . . ."

BODY ANGLE: leaning back
FACE: tense, angry
ARMS: wide movements
HANDS: raises finger, other
       hand as warning

Jack: ". . . there are a lot of benefits,   3.
but can't the base price be reduced?"

175

BODY ANGLE: leaning back and
away from Doug
FACE: tense, angry
ARMS: close to body
HANDS: stop gesture

4.   Jack: "That won't be necessary."

JACK REVISITED

Instead of losing the sale, Doug could have continued on into a close if the preceeding scene had gone like this:

THE SCENE

Doug (1): (open-handed gestures, slight lean forward.)

"Since you're understandably interested in price, Mr. Lowe, there's another benefit I'd like to mention. We have a special arrangement with First Colony Bank for obtaining excellent loan terms with a prepayment option."

Jack (2): (friendly, slight lean forward, taps desk.)

"It seems to me that you could still come down on that quote you gave me."

Doug (3): (maintains green posture, counts benefits on fingers.)

"I can assure you that this is the best price we've offered this year. For the benefits of (1) the automatic regulation system and (2) the override switch, you get increased safety for your employees. The same features give you (emphasis with voice) reduced repair costs. Therefore, this product will end up costing you less than a brand with only half the features over the long-run."

Jack (4): (leans forward, gestures with right hand.)

"I just have to be 100 percent sure that my boss won't tell me he knows of someone who got a lower price."

Doug (5): (unclasps his hands and sits upright from his listening posture, takes out a pad of paper and a pen.)

"Mr. Lowe, I'll be glad to give you the names of some of our satisfied customers so that you can assure your boss of the good deal you've made."

Jack (6): (smiles, gestures with hand.)

"OK! Just let me see your list and we can discuss the details."

Notice that much of this scene's dialogue is the same as Doug's poor sales call. The main difference is Doug's body language.

Below are the positive moves Doug made in this revised scene:

(1) Doug uses open gestures to encourage Jack's open body language. He acknowledges Jack's main concern about price and brings in an added benefit.

(2) Jack is not against a sale, but he wants to be sure he's getting the best price. He shows this by his green signals.

(3) Doug sees that Jack is not expressing a serious problem. He reassures Jack, maintains his own green signals, and visually as well as orally counts out the benefits Jack will receive with a purchase.

(4) Jack wants to buy but is concerned, uncertain about his boss's reaction. His move forward and serious look show Doug that he needs a little more reassurance.

(5) Doug uses the offer of satisfied customer referrals, reinforced by the physical act of writing them down right there to prove his interest and sincerity to Jack.

(6) Jack can't resist, feels sure that Doug is not the type of person who will give him a bad deal, and actually leads Doug into a close.

This is what the scene would look like (pages 178-179):

**Jack's Nonverbal
Signals**

BODY ANGLE: slightly forward
FACE: friendly, head tilted
ARMS: partially open
HANDS: one on hip, one on
                        desk

1.

Doug: ". . . there's another benefit
I'd like to mention."

BODY ANGLE: slightly forward
FACE: serious, listening
ARMS: open
HANDS: one on hip, one
                        gesturing

2.

Doug: "I can assure you. . . ."

BODY ANGLE: forward
FACE: serious
ARMS: close to body
HANDS: right hand gesturing

3.

Jack: "I just have to be 100% sure
that my boss won't tell me. . . ."

BODY ANGLE: upright
FACE: smiling
ARMS: open
HANDS: one on desk, other
using open-palmed
gestures

4.

Jack: "OK, just let me see your list. . . ."

BASICS FOR HANDLING OBJECTIONS

When your client states an objection, it is vital for you to manage your own and your client's nonverbal communications. If you can focus on the positive and turn aside negative comments without a head-to-head confrontation, your chances for a successful close are excellent.

During this phase of the call remember to:

- Continue to use green signals.
- Determine what type of objection your client is presenting—

TEASERS—client exhibits green signals, remains friendly. *Restate benefits.*

STALLS—Type #1, Passive, Client exhibits yellow signals, shows doubt or uncertainty. *Ask open questions, reassure the client, and address the hidden problem.*

Type #2, Active. Client exhibits green signals. *Restate benefits and ask for the order.*

PRICE—client exhibits yellow signals, shows aggressiveness or irritability. *Focus on dominant reasons for buying.*

LACK OF FUNDS—client exhibits yellow signals, seems concerned or worried. *Probe for information and offer alternatives.*

MISUNDERSTANDINGS—client exhibits yellow signals, seems defensive or confused. *Clarify complex information and restate benefits.*

PRODUCT PROBLEMS—client exhibits yellow signals, has a closed attitude. *Probe for specific concerns, provide proof of product value (quality, reliability, etc.).*

COMPANY PROBLEMS—client exhibits yellow or red signals, seems worried or doubtful. *Provide proof of company's good reputation (referrals, reports, etc.).*

SALES REP PROBLEMS—client exhibits yellow or red signals, is closed and uncooperative. *Ask for fair consideration, or offer to turn over the order to another sales rep.*

UNEXPECTED CHANGES—client states that company situation has changed. *Begin new needs analysis.*

- *Smile* and congratulate your buyer when you get the order.

CHAPTER **10**

Closing

Closing requires confidence and the conviction that your product or service is worth more than the price you're asking the prospect to pay. Top salespeople consistently show two behavior characteristics that get them the sale: the capacity to be friendly (empathy opens the sale) and the ability to be firm (ego drive closes the sale).

Although these attitudes may be present in every salesperson, they need to be applied in equal measure. Salespeople who are too friendly will get along fine with a customer, and will easily get a whole series of green signals, but may lack the inner strength to ask for the order. Salespeople who are too firm, on the other hand, may bulldoze through a sale, annoying the prospect and causing unnecessary changes from yellow to red signals.

The ability to be friendly and to create green signals is only a means to an end—the sale, the satisfied need, the happy customer, and your satisfied ego. To turn green signals into dollars, you need to balance this friendliness with firmness.

By following a basic two-part strategy of 1) disarming the customer, and 2) closing the sale, you will combine friendliness and firmness for sales success.

NONVERBAL SELLING STRATEGY

- Use the first trial close as soon as you notice steady green signals.
- Never close when the customer signals yellow.

181

- Express "buy from me" (green) signals during the close.
- Move closer to your customer by leaning forward; increase eye contact, and use head nods when closing.

VISUAL, AUDITORY, AND ACTION CLOSES

By the time you have reached the closing phase of your sales call you will know the type of language and information a client prefers. If you have been matching your vocabulary to your customer's, a close stressing this preference will seem natural.

Visual Closes

These are "show and tell" types of closes. Using pen and paper, you demonstrate in black and white how your prospect will benefit from purchasing your product. Prospects who prefer visual language are most likely to buy when you use the following visually oriented closes.

1. Summary Close

When the customer signals green, after listening to several benefit statements, look at the client, pick up a pen and a yellow pad, and say:

"I'd like us to take a moment to review what we've discussed (eye contact).

"We've agreed that our (product name) could help you (begin writing) increase production by 15 percent (watch for reaction—pause, then continue writing), reduce your repair costs (scan for signals), and, as we've agreed, (continue writing) allow you to cut the time for training new employees (smile, eye contact).

(Slowly turn your written summary to your prospect and say) "When would you like to see these benefits in your operation?"

2. Index Card Close

This close takes some advanced preparation. Take five 3 x 5 index cards and write one leading product feature and the corresponding customer benefit on each card (Example: Higher Grade Steel = longer lifetime, lower repair cost).

After you've explained all five features and benefits verbally during the sales call, take out the five index cards and put them face down on the table saying:

> "I'd like to show you how you can win by betting on this hand (smile). (Turn up card #1 saying) By betting on a higher grade steel, you'll win lower repair costs.
>
> (Turn up card #2) "By betting on lower fuel consumption with our turbo diesel engine, you'll win as much as $8 per hour of operation . . .
>
> (After you turn up the last card and continue to receive green signals, close with) "The best thing about this hand is that it takes only your handshake and an autograph to make us both winners (extend hand, then write up the order)."

If you prefer a simpler version you can say:

> "What kind of down payment did you have in mind for this winning hand?"

If you receive yellow signals as you turn up the cards, change your approach and ask:

> "How do you see the benefits of this winning hand?"

This gives the prospect a chance to express his or her concern prior to making the decision.

3. Objective Evaluation Close

This close involves a written summary of the pros and cons of the buying decision. After you've used several trial closes, but have received no firm commitment, look in your customer's eyes saying:

> "I'd like to show you how you can objectively look at the reasons for and against making a decision. (Pause, pick up a piece of paper saying) This paper can show us the reasons for (write a plus sign on the top left-hand corner, look at customer, smile) and against (look at paper, write a minus sign on the top right-hand corner) owning the product at this time.
>
> (Pause, draw a solid vertical line to divide the paper into two parts, saying) "Here on the left side we'll show the benefits that we've

already discussed such as (begin writing) higher productivity (look at customer, nod head), lower downtime, no need for special tools (look at customer, smile), and the fact that you'll save approximately 14 percent on operating costs per hour compared to the model you're using at this time (eye contact, pause). Which one of these benefits would be the most important one for you?"

Now wait for your customer's reply. After you've discussed this "best benefit," continue:

"Of course we could go on with this list, but before we do that, I'd like you to look at this and (indicate right side of paper) help me with the reasons that speak against owning this product now (eye contact)."

In most situations, the customer will either grin and buy your product or tell you:

"The main reason against buying now is the . . ."

Your next step is to isolate the objection by saying:

"Is that the only reason that prevents you from owning this money-making product?"

If the answer is "Yes," handle the objection using the information from Chapter 9 and move on to the close.

4. Traditional, Assumptive Close

As you make your product presentation, place your order form next to you, visible to the customer. You nonverbally indicate your intentions to get the order during this call. As you move on in your presentation, ask qualifying questions such as:

"If you were to order today, would two dozen cartons be enough?" (As you receive the answer, write 2 dozen on your order form) Or you may ask:

"Do you have a preference for the color as shown in this brochure?" (Write color preference on the order form.)

As you gradually complete the order form, you only need to ask:

"Would you please confirm what we've discussed (hand over pen) so we can get to work on this right away?"

Auditory Closes

Prospects who prefer an auditory vocabulary and information are most likely to buy from you when they hear these closes.

1. The "Yes-Set" Close

This close involves making statements or asking questions to which the only reasonable answer is "Yes."

> "Do you like the quality of this storage building?"
> "Yes."
> "Do you like the colors you selected earlier?"
> "Yes."
> "Can you get the financing?"
> "Yes."
> "Then it sounds as though we can go ahead with putting it on paper."
> "Yes."

The repeated "Yes" mode has a powerful psychological impact on the auditory customer. Each additional "Yes" increases the unconscious desire to repeat the positive internal experience of the "Yes" sound. Top sales producers can benefit from this phenomenon by obtaining several "Yes" responses before asking for the order.

2. The Extra Incentive Close

Make your offer sound irresistible by stating with excitement in your voice:

> "You'll be pleased to hear that this week we double our normal bonus from two extra cases to four. How does that sound to you?"

Or:

> "We have only two units left (hand-to-chest gesture) and the new shipment won't be sold at this low price." (Lower voice level, use eye contact.)

Or:

> "This week we're including free installation (pause) and a two-hour training course for your personnel with the purchase of a new system (smile)."

3. Alternate Choice Close

To lead your customer from a thinking mode to a decision mode, you can ask a number of questions about the details of your proposal such as:

"Does the lease plan sound good to you or would you like to hear about owning this equipment?"

Or:

"What sounds best to you—should we have our technicians call on you to install the equipment, or can your maintenance crew ring up some extra savings for you by following the simple installation instructions included in the owner's manual?"

Or:

"Which color sounds more appealing to you—brown or blue?"

Or:

"Would you like to hear about our special weekend delivery schedule, or does saving on rush charges and waiting until Monday sound better?"

4. Approval Close

Verbally summarize the product benefits you've explained previously:

"It sounds as though we're in harmony on these points. We've talked about the satisfactory delivery schedule, and you recall the benefits of the reduced workload and the $320 savings per month on operating expenses (smile). I can see that this deal is music to your ears!" (Wait for a response.)

Or:

"Since we both want to avoid hearing more problems from your assembly line supervisor, and since we've agreed to extend our warranty by 6 months, it sounds as if we can start writing up the order."

Action Closes

Action-oriented prospects show a number of "I am ready to buy" signals such as:

- Nodding head.
- Making physical contact with you (i.e., placing hand on your shoulder).
- Hand-rubbing.
- Grabbing a pen for writing.
- Walking around your product, stroking parts of it (feel finish, adjust seat, open trunk, etc.)

Use these signals as a cue for the final close.

1. Future Action Close

Describe the benefits your customer will experience through owning your product at some point in the future.

"Mr. Smith, as a manager who expects people and equipment to go the extra mile, I can see you standing at your new mining site a year from now.

"There are 14 new trucks, each hauling 85 tons of coal during two eight-hour shifts every day of the week.

"You take your computer and check the maintenance record for the past year and as you glance at the printout you'll jump up and down because you've exceeded 95 percent availability for twelve months in a row (pause). Isn't this the kind of turnaround situation you're expecting from this purchase?"

2. Customer as Sales Assistant Close

Action-oriented buyers love to give you a hand. Ask them to do things for you such as:

"Mrs. Grey, would you please hold this end of the tape measure so I can go and find out exactly how far your pool should be from this fence?"

Or:

"Mr. Dunkin, could you take this book and help me to select the kind of monthly benefits you'll want to receive from your policy?"

Or:

"Mr. Wiley, do you have a dollar bill?"

"Yes."

"May I ask you to turn one over to me just for half a minute?"

"OK, here is a dollar bill."

"Thank you. (Pause.) Now, how would you feel if I came into your office every hour and asked you to give me a dollar? Eight times a day, every day of the week?"

"These are hard to come by, I wouldn't like it one bit!"

"I understand how you feel. You wouldn't want me to take away $40 a week from you. But that's exactly the amount you'll be paying a week in operating costs by leaving things the way they are. By using our model 211, you'll save $40 a week. That's like my giving you a dollar every hour on the hour." (Hand dollar bill back to customer.)

3. Change of Scene Close

Prospects who use action-oriented language respond well to your leadership. For example, if you've made a product presentation outside and realize that the prospect is still undecided, you could say:

"Mrs. Long, let's take a moment and walk over to the office (start moving, continue talking as you walk). I'd like you to take a look at two large photographs of similar designs you've seen here which I think will really suit your specific needs."

A business consultant involved in selling a series of seminars tried to close a sale in a client's office and the prospect was hesitant and kept stalling. The consultant stood up unexpectedly saying:

"Let's go over to the conference room to see if the facilities are suitable for the type of meeting we have outlined in our proposal."

The prospect followed and, once removed from his own power base, turned into a very cooperative and helpful buyer. No new features or benefits were discussed in the conference room, the consultant simply "approved" the facilities and got the order by saying:

"I think we can use this room, providing we can use our own video equipment."

"No problem, here are some extra electrical outlets."

"When would you like us to conduct our first session?"

"Well, would you be able to do it on the first of next month?"
"Is that the date you want us to start our 12 sessions?"
"Yes."
"OK, we'll start on the first."

Note that action-oriented buyers sometimes need to be moved physically to close the sale.

4. Pack-Up and Leave Close

In some situations, your customer may be ready for the purchase, but needs a gentle push to make the decision. You, on the other hand, know that too much assertiveness may be counterproductive at this time.

On this occasion, you can begin to pack up your sales literature, order forms, and samples, leading the customer to believe that you are on your way out the door. You'll soon see your prospect's defenses being lowered. As you notice the signals, turn to the customer and refocus on the dominant buying motive.

"Dr. Hall, this thought just occurred to me. Is the only reason that prevents you from using this electronic blood analyzer the tight budget situation caused by your newly added X-ray room?"
"Yes."
"What if financing were not a problem at all, would you go ahead with the purchase?"
"Of course."
"If I could show you a way to combine both investments into one refinancing package so that your monthly payments would be about the same, would you be interested?"
"Yes."

Save a good product feature, a special finance offer, an extra incentive, or a new creative solution to the client's problem for the pack-up and leave close. Your moving closer to the customer's door will lower his or her resistance to a successful comeback and final close.

A SAMPLE CLOSE

Lou Greer has hit it off quite well with his client Mel Banks. Lou proceeds to his close after he answers Mel's questions about his product.

THE SCENE

Lou (1): (green signals, open-palmed gestures.)

"Because of your needs for availability and high monthly volume requirements during peak periods, a contract with our company will improve your competitive standing enormously, and in a very short time."

Mel (2): (nods, smiles, leans slightly back and away from Lou, fiddles with his fingers.)

"Yes, I think your company is what we're looking for."

Lou (3): (steeples his hands.)

"Can I put you down for 20 or 30 boxes to start?"

Mel (4): (leans back a bit farther, looks away from Lou, frown and wrinkles brow.)

"Before we get anything down on paper here, I've got to know what my return guarantees are—just how flexible are you in this area?"

Lou (5): (realizes he is steepling, opens hands, nods to Mel as he is speaking. Now he leans forward, uses his hands to count out options.)

"Of course you want to know your guarantees. With our flexible order policy, you can return any overstock that is not sold within 90 days and exchange it for any other item in our catalog. Let's say that you order 40 boxes today (gestures with fingers) and end up with seven unsold after 90 days. You just call me, or our warehouse manager Bill Curtis, and we'll let you choose a more saleable substitute from our catalog."

Mel (6): (has cocked his head to listen, lightly grasping chair arms.)

"Are you sure all of this won't get my account completely confused at your office?"

Lou (7): (uses open-palms gestures.)

"I'll be handling your account on a regular basis Mr. Banks. If you ever have a question about your order, I'll be glad to handle the matter personally."
(hand to chest.)

Mel (8): (nods, smiles.)

"That seems fair enough. When can I get my first shipment delivered?"

Lou (9): (smiles, looks confident.)

"As soon as we get the paper work filled out, I'll call in your order to the warehouse and make sure that it gets here by Thursday."

Mel (10): (smiles, leans forward to shake hands.)

"That's great! Let's get this thing on the road."

Here is how Lou managed his own and his client's signals to close the deal:

(1) Lou begins his close by summing up Mel's dominant needs as well as his product's major benefits, while using green signals.

(2) Mel is beginning to show very subtle yellow signals as he leans back slightly and fiddles with his fingers. There is evidently something on his mind and Lou needs to discover what it is and eliminate any problems before continuing on with his close.

(3) Lou is concentrating on his close and steeples his hands without realizing it. He also misses the yellow signals Mel is sending out. Perhaps he is distracted by Mel's smile and his nodding.

(4) Mel increases the intensity of his yellow signals by leaning farther back and looking away. He is not sure that Lou's company can keep his complicated ordering needs correct.

(5) Lou realizes that Mel is sending out warning signals, and also sees that he is steepling his hands—a dominant gesture that can kill the deal if not checked. He changes to an evaluative posture and deals with Mel's concern.

(6) Mel loosens up but is still not sending out green signals. He is probably still reacting to Lou's poor body language.

(7) Lou sees that he does not have Mel's complete trust yet, so he reassures Mel that he will handle any problems and uses open-palms and hand-to-chest gestures to reinforce his sincerity.

(8) Mel relaxes, and goes back to using green signals. He is now confident that Lou is interested in keeping his orders in line.

(9) Lou makes sure that Mel remains open to a final close by giving him one more benefit—personal, quick service for a fast delivery.

(10) Mel is happy to close the deal and initiates a handshake to finalize the agreement.

Here is a view of Lou and Mel's nonverbal communications during this scene (pages 192-195):

1.

     Lou: ". . . a contract with our
          company will improve your competitive
          standing enormously, and in a very
          short time."

NONVERBAL SIGNALS

LOU

BODY ANGLE: forward
FACE: smiling, friendly
ARMS: open
HANDS: open-palmed gesture,
      resting on knee
LEGS: open

MEL

BODY ANGLE: slightly forward
FACE: smiling, friendly
ARMS: open
HANDS: open-palmed gesture,
      resting on chair arm
LEGS: open

2.

Lou: "Can I put you down for
20 or 30 boxes to start?"

NONVERBAL SIGNALS

LOU

BODY ANGLE: leaning back and
      to the side
FACE: smiling, superior look
ARMS: close to body
HANDS: steepling
LEGS: one tucked under chair

MEL

BODY ANGLE: upright, turned
      away from Lou
FACE: frown, annoyance
ARMS: close to body, pushed
      behind chair
HANDS: pushing on chair arm,
      covering groin
LEGS: one tucked under chair

3.

Lou: "With our flexible order policy,
you can return any overstock that
is not sold within 90 days. . . ."

NONVERBAL SIGNALS

LOU

BODY ANGLE: forward
FACE: friendly, smiling
ARMS: open
HANDS: open-palmed, using
       fingers to illustrate
       benefits
LEGS: open

MEL

BODY ANGLE: upright
FACE: serious, evaluating
ARMS: close to body, back
      against chair
HANDS: grasping chair arms
LEGS: open

4.

Mel: "That's great. Let's get
this thing on the road."

NONVERBAL SIGNALS

LOU

BODY ANGLE: forward
FACE: smiling, friendly
ARMS: open
HANDS: shaking hands
LEGS: open

MEL

BODY ANGLE: forward
FACE: smiling, friendly
ARMS: open
HANDS: shaking hands
LEGS: open

BASICS FOR A SUCCESSFUL CLOSE

When you have used 100 percent of your communications abilities during a sales call, your close will follow automatically. Getting to the close means that you have managed your own and your client's body language effectively. To conclude your meeting successfully you will:

- Never begin a close unless you have a green signal from your client.
- Continue to use your own green signals and maintain good eye contact.
- Select a close that suits your client based on his preference for visual, auditory, or action words and information.
- Immediately redirect your approach if the client signals yellow during your close—ask open questions, restate benefits, and continue to respond with green signals.
- Smile and thank the client for the order.
- Reassure the buyer that the order is only the beginning of a long-term relationship.
- Schedule a follow-up call to check on how your sale has improved the buyer's situation (ask for leads and testimonials!).

CHAPTER 11

Conclusion

Sales success is a combination of three factors: knowledge, skills, and motivation. Studying this book will add to your sales knowledge, but knowledge alone is worthless, unless you use what you learn. To translate knowledge into action skills, you need to practice, make mistakes, learn from them, and grow. New action skills will increase your confidence tremendously and boost your motivation to an all-time high.

If you haven't started your program of nonverbal selling power yet, here are some pointers on how to use this book as a guideline for improving your sales techniques.

• Watch what people do with their bodies every day for a week. You may want to use the five nonverbal communication channels as a starter—concentrate on Body Angle on Monday, Faces on Tuesday, Arms on Wednesday, Hands on Thursday, and Leg Postures on Friday.

• Improve your nonverbal observation skills by watching TV talk shows, such as Merv Griffin and Johnny Carson, with the sound off. Note the guest's initial seating position (usually legs crossed away from the host!), and the hand gestures (the confident guest uses frequent, open gestures). Also note the "mirroring" effect when both people are on the same wavelength (positive or negative).

• Imitate gestures you've seen in a client's office, after the call, in order to "feel and understand" what your customer has expressed nonverbally.

197

- Work on your listening posture, your opening seating position, and your ability to express green signals no matter what objections you hear.

- Ask your colleagues to role-play in small groups with you. Form triads (3 people per group)—one plays the role of the buyer, one plays the seller, and the third acts as observer. Learn to apply new techniques in a safe, controlled situation before you use them on a real customer. (You'll soon learn what works for you and what doesn't.)

- Develop a "nonverbal call report" diary to use after your sales call. Write down what type of nonverbal signals you used on calls where you got the order and what signals you used when you lost a sale. Your own observations may be a bit too self-critical, but soon you'll see a pattern of success in your approach. Follow it. Your goal is to identify the characteristics of your own best performance and repeat them often.

- Finally, learn how to use verbal and nonverbal selling power simultaneously. Start by using persuasive eye contact as you translate product features into customer benefits (Feature—look at brochure, Benefit—look into customer's eyes). Apply one new skill each day. Practice, practice, practice.

You have been reacting to nonverbal communication signals and sending out your own body language all your life. Responding to these signals in a positive manner, instead of reacting to them in a negative way, will provide you with an enormous competitive edge. You've just added 93 percent to your communications potential. Putting *Nonverbal Selling Power* to work will turn that potential into profit.

Bibliography

Books

Birdwhistell, Ray. *Kinesics and Context*, Philadelphia: University of Pennsylvania, 1970.

Cooper, Ken. *Nonverbal Communication for Business Success*, New York: Amacom, 1979

Davis, Flora. *Inside Intuition: What We Know about Nonverbal Communication*, New York: McGraw-Hill, 1973.

Druckman, Daniel, et. al. *Nonverbal Communication: Survey, Theory, and Research*, Beverly Hills: Sage Publications, 1982.

Ekman, Paul, and Friesen, Wallace. *Unmasking the Face*, Englewood Cliffs, N.J.: Prentice-Hall, Inc., 1978.

Gumperz, John. *Discourse Strategies*, New York: Cambridge University Press, 1982.

Lamb, Warren, and Watson, Elizabeth. *Body Code: The Meaning of Movement*, London: Routledge & Kegan Paul Ltd., 1979.

Knapp, Mark L. *Nonverbal Communication in Human Interaction*, New York: Holt, Rinehart & Winston, 1972.

Leathers, Dale. *Nonverbal Communication Systems*, Boston: Allyn & Bacon Inc., 1976.

Mehrabian, Albert. *Nonverbal Communication*, Chicago: Aldine, 1972.

Mehrabian. *Silent Messages*, Belmont, Ca.: Wadsworth Publishing Co., 1971.

Millar, Dan, and Millar, Frank. *Messages and Myths: Understanding Interpersonal Communications*, New York: Alfred Publishing Co., 1976.

Nierenberg, Gerard I. and Calero, Henry H. *How to Read a Person Like a Book*, New York: Hawthorn, 1971.

Reynolds, William. *Nonverbal Communication*, New York: Random House, 1973.

Scheflen, Albert E., M.D. *Body Language and Social Order: Communication as Behavioral Control*, Prentice-Hall, Inc., Englewood Cliffs, N.J.: 1972.

Scheflen. *How Behavior Means*, New York: Gordon & Breach, 1973.

Steere, David A., Ph.D. *Bodily Expressions in Psychotherapy*, New York: Brunner/Mazel Inc., 1982.

Whiteside, Robert L. *Face Language*, New York: Frederick Fell Publishing, Inc., 1974.

Wolfgang, Aaron (ed). *Nonverbal Behavior: Applications and Cultural Implications*, New York: Academic Press, 1979.

Zunin, Leonard, M.D., and Zunin, Natalie. *Contact: The First Four Minutes*, New York: Ballantine Books, 1972.

Articles

Bonoma, Thomas V., and Felder, Leonard C. "Nonverbal Communication in Marketing: Toward a Communicational Analysis" *Journal of Marketing Research*, May 1977.

Doctoroff, Michael. "Nonverbal Communication—a Key to Executive Success" *International Management*, Nov. 1977.

Fast, Julius (interviewed). "How Well Do You Read Body Language?" *Sales & Marketing Management Magazine*, Dec. 1970.

Gschwandtner, Gerhard. "Traffic Signals to the Buyer's Mind: How to Read Your Prospect's Body Language" *Personal Selling Power (PSP)*, Jan./Feb., 1984.

Jason, Kathrine. "Smile Power" (studies by James Laird) *Omni*, Jan. 1984.

McCaskey, Michael B. "The Hidden Messages Managers Send" *Harvard Business Review*, Nov./Dec. 1979.

Rosenthal, R., et. al. "The Language Without Words" *Psychology Today*, Sept. 1974.

Sheridan, Johan H. "Are You a Victim of Nonverbal 'Vibes'?" *Industry Week*, July 10, 1978.

Sutton, Suzy. "Gestures—Do They Sell or Sabotage You?" *PSP*, Nov./Dec. 1982.

Thompson, Jacqueline. "Image Doctors: They Can Spruce Up Your Career" *PSP*, May/June 1982.

York, Brenda. "Design Your Image of Success" *PSP*, Oct. 1983.

Audio-Visual Sales Training Course

Gschwandtner, Gerhard. *The Languages of Selling*, Gerhard Gschwandtner & Associates, 1127 International Parkway, Suite 102, Fredericksburg, Va. 22405, 703/752-7000. Complete sales training course with comprehensive leader's guide, participants' workbooks and 160 slides. Also available on video.